Children's Book of
MAGIC

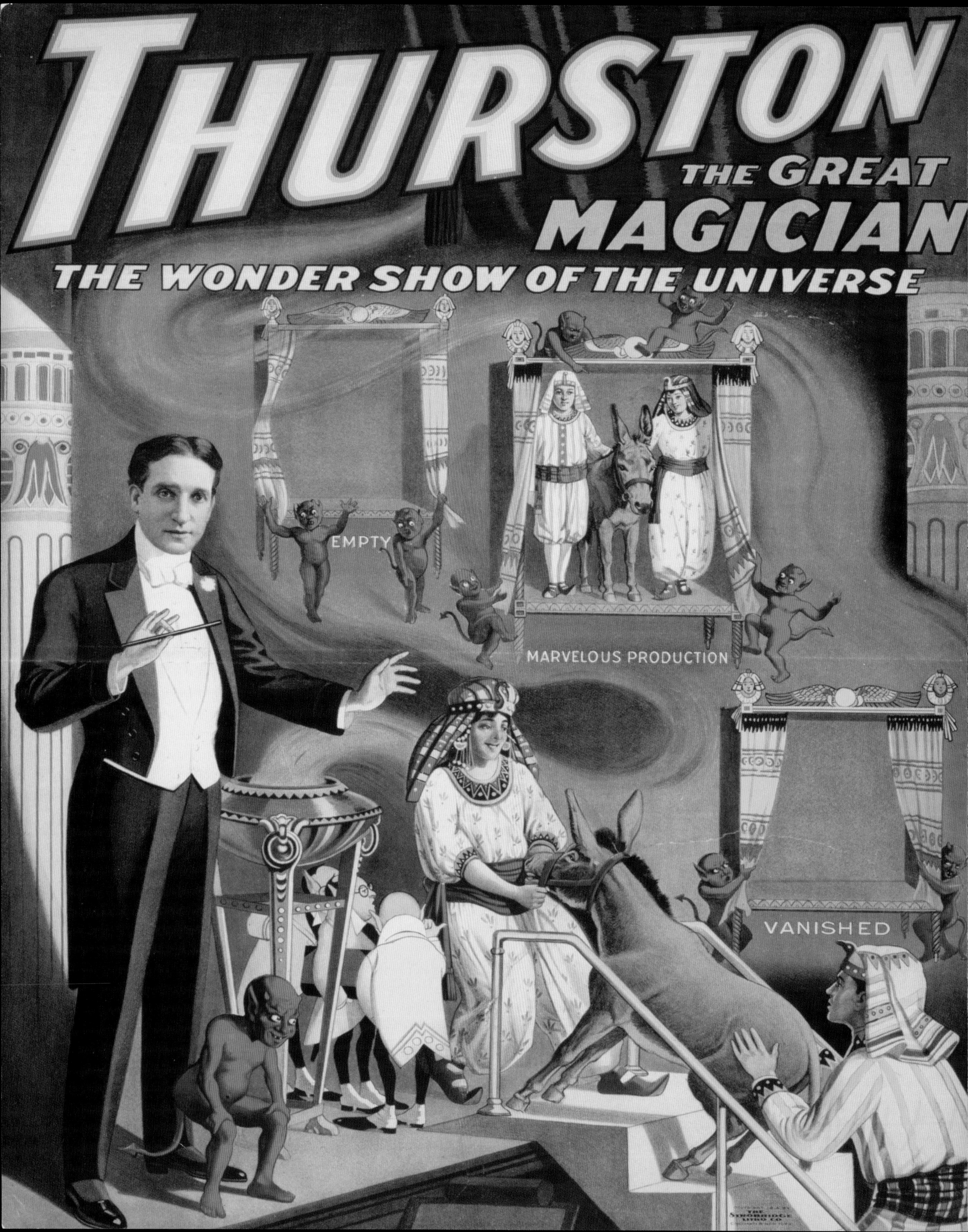
THURSTON
THE GREAT
MAGICIAN
THE WONDER SHOW OF THE UNIVERSE
EMPTY
MARVELOUS PRODUCTION
VANISHED

CONTENTS

WHAT IS MAGIC?

Today we think of magic as the art of performing illusions, making the impossible seem possible, and the unbelievable believable. But that wasn't always the case. The idea of magic has actually been around for thousands of years, it just meant different things to different people.

Magic has always been about **mystery**. That mystery used to come in the form of spells, rituals, witches, and wizards, but today it's used to bring us joy and wonder.

This book will allow you to enjoy that mystery by teaching you **fantastic tricks** to try on your friends and family. By the time you're finished, you'll be able to make objects appear and disappear, move and change, and seem to have the power to read minds.

But that's just the beginning. You'll also learn about **history's greatest magicians**, the secrets of sleight of hand, the power of misdirection, and much more.

The aim of this book is to start young magicians on a journey to become **the magicians of tomorrow**. So turn the pages and start creating a little mystery of your own.

MAGIC AND THE ANCIENT WORLD

People in the ancient world believed magic could help them tell the future, appease the gods, and lay curses on other people. Some of this magic involved calling on the gods for help, other spells would work on their own. We know about this magic by studying ancient texts and artifacts.

Sibylline books
Around 500BCE King Tarquin of Rome bought three **books of prophecies** from a priestess. Later generations of Romans consulted the books whenever Rome was in danger. They were last used in 405CE.

The cave paintings at Lascaux, France.

Cave magic
About 17,000 years ago humans living in Western Europe painted pictures of the animals they hunted on the walls of caves. The paintings may have been part of a magical ritual aimed at **improving hunting success**.

A human skull decorated with blue and black stones to look like Tezcatlipoca.

Tezcatlipoca
The ancient Aztecs worshipped many gods, one of whom was Tezcatlipoca – the god of the night, of storms, of jaguars, and of the future. Aztec priests would **eat a ritual meal** in front of a statue of Tezcatlipoca to try to see into the future.

I Ching

In China the 3,000 year old system of I Ching is used in an attempt to **tell the future** by using a set of sacred texts. Three coins are thrown six times to produce a number, which is looked up in the book to give answers to questions.

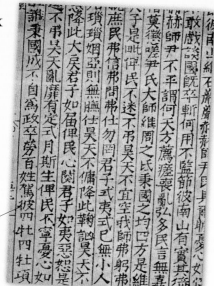

A page from the book of I Ching.

Battle of Thermopylae

The Spartans fought the Persians at the Battle of Thermopylae in 480BCE. For two days the Spartan seer **Megastius** sacrificed a goat and predicted victory. On the third day he predicted death. By nightfall he and all the other Spartans were dead.

FACT

The Romans wrote curses on tablets and threw them into sacred rivers or lakes. Many have been found in the hot springs at Bath, England, sacred to the goddess Sulis-Minerva.

Book of the Dead

Ancient Egyptians were buried with magical spells written on papyrus and illustrated with **pictures of the gods**. This "Book of the Dead" contained spells to help the dead person talk to the gods and gain a comfortable afterlife.

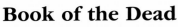

SORCERY, CONJURING, AND WIZARDS

In years past, sorcerers and wizards claimed to use magic to predict the future, talk to spirits, and gain special powers. Some used their abilities to help people, others used them for selfish or evil purposes. Many wizards use objects such as drums, dolls, or wands to help with their rituals.

Old Mother Shipton

Born in a cave in Yorkshire, England, around 1488, Ursula Southell made many **prophecies about the future**. Some came true, but her most famous: "The world to an end shall come in eighteen hundred and eighty one" obviously did not!

John Dee

An adviser to Queen Elizabeth I, John Dee lived from 1527 to 1609. He was a mathematician, spy, astronomer, and magician who claimed to have **talked with spirits** to ask them questions. Many historians believe he was the first Agent 007, the codename of the character James Bond.

John Dee signed his letters with two circles that signified secret eyes.

The Brahan Seer predicted "worldwide chaos" if five bridges were built over the River Ness. A month after a fifth bridge was built, World War II broke out.

The Brahan Seer

Coinneach Odhar lived at Brahan, Scotland, in the 17th century. He worked for the Earl of Seaforth, making **predictions about the future** or telling Seaforth what his friends and enemies were doing many miles away.

A sami drum used by a Scandinavian shaman.

Sangoma

The sangoma of southern Africa use medicinal herbs, spells, and **rituals** to cure disease, find lost cattle, tell the future, and to help with childbirth. Since 2007 sangomas have been registered with the government in South Africa.

Shamans

A shaman is a person who goes into a trance during a ritual in order to contact spirits, gods, or demons. Shamans exist to this day in parts of the world, and many use a drum to help them communicate with the spirits.

Merlin gives advice to King Arthur in many adventures.

Wizards in literature

Medieval stories tell of Merlin, the wizard who helped King Arthur. More recent books and films have featured wizards such as Harry Potter, Gandalf the Grey, and the Wizard of Oz.

FACT

Voodoo dolls or "gris gris" are more often used to bring good luck than injury. The pins are used to attach pictures of food, money, or medicine to the doll to give the real person the benefit of that object.

King Arthur got his magical sword Excalibur from the mystical Lady of the Lake.

STUDYING ALCHEMY

Alchemists believed it was possible to turn metals into gold by examining the properties of various materials, chemicals, and objects. Alchemists thought their work would lead to eternal life or magical powers. It never did, but they did make various important scientific discoveries.

Alexandria

The origins of alchemy can be traced to the ancient Egyptian city of Alexandria. It was founded in 331BCE and became a famous centre of learning. Alexandria was home to the world's biggest library.

Jabir ibn Hayyan

Born around 722CE, Jabir ibn Hayyan spent most of his life in Iran. He studied **distillation, evaporation, and crystallization**. More than 3,000 books are said to have been written by him, but most were written by some of his students.

Alexandria's great library was full of important texts.

Many great thinkers went to Alexandria to study alchemy.

Hermes Trismegistus

The ancient Greeks believed that alchemy was invented by the god **Hermes the Thrice Great**. Hermes was also said to have invented astrology, writing, and magic.

Roger Bacon

The English monk Roger Bacon spent years experimenting with chemicals and materials. He is most famous for inventing the **magnifying glass**, and was imprisoned for several years after the Church disapproved of his work.

Bacon is said to have developed an early form of gunpowder.

FACT

Alchemists believed that a mystical substance called "The philosopher's stone" was the secret to being able to turn metals such as lead into gold. It was also thought to be able to allow alchemists to live forever.

Many of Newton's works on alchemy were lost in a fire.

Isaac Newton

The English scientist Isaac Newton is often considered to be the greatest mathematician and scientist who ever lived. He **discovered gravity** and several other laws about the Universe. He also studied as an alchemist, but his family hid this secret work until Newton's notebooks were published in 1932.

Muhammad ibn Zakariya al-Razi

This Persian alchemist was born in 854CE. He worked as a doctor, but spent a lot of his spare time on alchemy. Al Razi was once believed to be able to turn copper into silver and **iron into gold**. He wrote a book about alchemy called *The Secret of all Secrets*.

WITCHCRAFT AND THE OCCULT

The occult means "knowledge of the supernatural". Witches are women who claim to use supernatural forces to cast spells. Some witches call on gods to help them, others say they can control spirits. White witches try to use their powers to help people, but the aim of black magic is to cause sickness or death.

Macbeth and the witches

According to legend, Macbeth, Lord of Glamis, Scotland, met three witches who predicted he would become first the Lord of Cawdor, then King of Scotland, and finally die in battle. **All this became true**. The tale is retold in Shakespeare's play "Macbeth".

The Devil

In Christian religion the Devil is the enemy of God and the **creator of all evil**. Witches were believed to worship the Devil at secret ceremonies. Some people believed witchcraft was an organised religion that spread across all Europe.

Burnt at the stake

In many European countries witchcraft was illegal and the **punishment was death**. Between 1550 and 1680 about 80,000 people were executed as witches, many of them burnt at the stake.

The Salem Witch Trials

In 1692 two girls in the town of Salem, Massachusetts, USA, had fits that were **blamed on witchcraft**. Three women were arrested but the suspicions spread and eventually 20 people were executed as witches.

FACT

Modern witch costumes feature tall, pointed hats with a brim, and a long black dress. These are based on the 17th century costume usually worn by elderly widows.

Cunning folk

In the 18th and 19th centuries there were many "cunning" men and women who used **herbs and potions** to cure sickness. They also used hypnosis, threats, and promises to convince people that they had special powers and were involved with many occultist texts.

Wicca

Wicca is a religion that originated in England and has now spread to many countries. People describe Wicca as good and natural magic and associate it with **white witchcraft**

MYSTICISM

The practice of seeking a special relationship with a god through ritual or prayer is called mysticism. Some mystics claim to use special powers, whereas others say it is their closeness to a god that gives them powers over other people.

Eleusinian Mysteries

In the ancient Greek town of Eleusis there was a temple to the harvest goddess Demeter. Strange, secret rituals and events called "The Mysteries" took place in the temple. Nobody who took part in the rituals was ever **allowed to say** what happened.

Kabbalah

The teachings of Kabbalah began as a branch of the religion Judaism. Kabbalists say the Bible and other writings have **hidden meanings** that can only be found by long, secret study.

Sadhu

The Sadhu are holy men in the Hindu religion. They give up all their personal possessions to study purity and ways to **serve the gods**. Female sadhu are called sadhvi.

Nirvana

In the Buddhist religion, Nirvana is the state of purity achieved by holy people who have managed to leave behind all human desires, fears, and delusions. Such people achieve **stillness and peace** with God.

Mithraism

Roman worshippers of the god Mithras met in underground temples, ate ritual meals, and exchanged a secret handshake. Mithras promised **eternal life** to his worshippers.

Mystical Theology

Christian mysticism seeks to find contact with God through going into a **trance** or prolonged prayer. In the 16th century St Teresa of Avila is said to have gained deep theological insights while in a trance.

New Age thinking

Since around 1950 some people have looked to astrology, alchemy, and aspects of Hinduism or Buddhism to create the **New Age concept**. They pursue peace, serenity and oneness with nature.

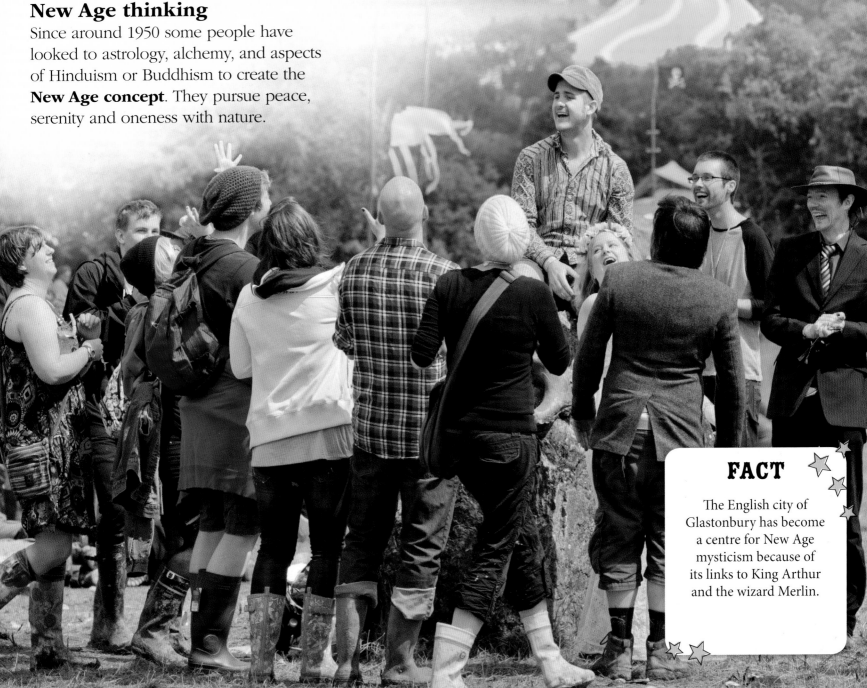

FACT

The English city of Glastonbury has become a centre for New Age mysticism because of its links to King Arthur and the wizard Merlin.

THE RISE OF STAGE MAGIC

Up until the 1800s many people still thought of magic as something supernatural. That all changed with the emerging popularity of stage magic. For the first time, large audiences caught a glimpse of what illusions could be, and would fill huge theatres seeking entertainment and mystery.

FACT

During the 20th century television helped make magic popular. But this wouldn't have happened without the work of the talented stage magicians who came before.

An angled pane of glass projected an image of a ghost.

Smoke and mirrors

The expression "smoke and mirrors" means **cleverly deceiving people**, and it's something stage magicians are famous for. The "Pepper's ghost" illusion involved a ghostly figure appearing on stage. To do this, John Henry Pepper had to design a special stage with a hidden glass panel and a complicated lighting setup.

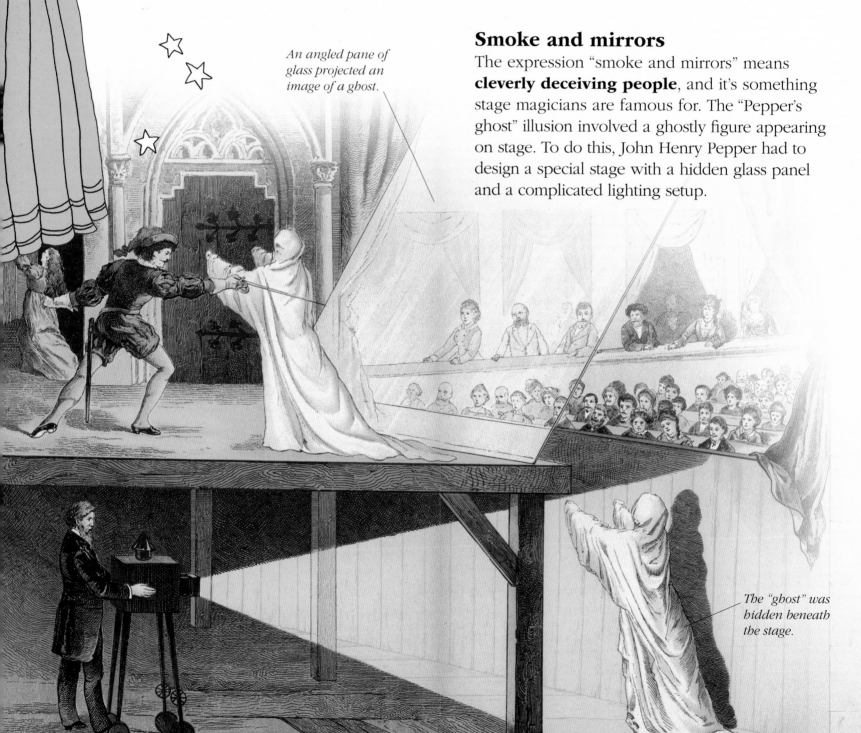

The "ghost" was hidden beneath the stage.

Viva Las Vegas

Stage magic is still very popular today. Magician's such as Penn and Teller, Criss Angel, Lance Burton, and David Copperfield regularly sell out shows in Las Vegas, USA. The city's large number of casinos, with their **bright lights and big stages,** are the perfect place for tourists looking to be entertained.

The Father of Modern Magic

Jean Eugène Robert-Houdin was one of the first magicians to perform his tricks in front of large audiences. Some of the tricks he invented more than **150 years ago** were so advanced they are still performed today. This is why he is known as "The Father of Modern Magic".

Stage magicians would dazzle crowds with an array of props.

Crowd pleasers

Having access to a stage gave magicians a new range of tools such as trap doors and mirrors to work with. This allowed them to be more creative than ever, and as shows became more popular, **costumes, props, animals, and music** were added. Magic grew so popular that magicians travelled all over the world performing in sold-out theatres.

Jean Eugène Robert-Houdin

1805-1871

"A magician is an actor playing the part of a magician".

Often described as the Father of Modern Magic, Robert-Houdin understood the importance of putting on a show. Unlike magicians before him, who dressed more like wizards in capes and flowing robes, Robert-Houdin wore formal evening dress, just as many magicians do today. He was also one of the first magicians to make use of the recent discoveries of electricity and scientific inventions.

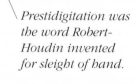

Prestidigitation was the word Robert-Houdin invented for sleight of hand.

Theatre of magic

Robert-Houdin acquired the use of an elegant theatre in Paris for his spectacular shows. As well as his magical tricks, he displayed **automata** (early mechanical robots), clockwork dolls and models that delighted his audiences. His shows became so popular that even the French king attended.

Second sight

Robert-Houdin's son Emile was a skilled magician in his own right. As part of a double act the duo performed a **mind reading** trick where Robert-Houdin would hold items up in front of the audience and a blindfolded Emile would identify and describe each one.

The duo devised a complicated code of thousands of words and phrases.

Emile could identify more than 100 different objects while blindfolded.

Ethereal suspension

Trained as a clockmaker, Robert-Houdin was fascinated by mechanical objects and their inner workings. But he also had a **scientific mind**. He used his knowledge of the newly discovered gas ether to trick the audience into believing it could make a body so light it would float in the air.

FACT

One of Robert-Houdin's tricks was "The Marvellous Orange Tree". He would produce an orange tree and magically make it blossom and then bear fruit. The oranges were passed around to the audience.

MAGICAL EFFECTS

There are thousands of magic tricks and illusions to learn, so it can seem a little overwhelming for beginners. However, each one is really a twist on one or more of these effects.

4 In **prediction** and **divination** tricks a magician anticipates the outcome of an event.

1 **Production** involves making something appear. It can be anything – even a person!

3 **Levitation** is about defying gravity by making something or someone float or appear to fly. A variation of this is called **suspension**.

2 **Vanishing** is the opposite of production. Here the goal is to make something or someone disappear.

5 **Transformation** is simply turning one thing into another. It can have very impressive results.

7 **Escapology** is when a performer is placed in a restraining device such as handcuffs and has to get free.

TRANSFORMATION
5

RESTORATION
6

ESCAPOLOGY
7

TELEPORTATION
8

6 **Restoration** is when a magician takes a broken object and returns it to its former self.

8 **Teleportation**, or transference, is moving something from one place to another seemingly by magic.

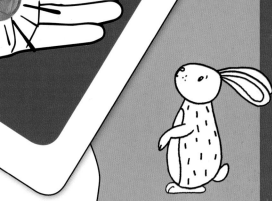

PRODUCTION

One of the most common effects is making an object or person appear. A simple example could be a coin or bunch of flowers being pulled from thin air, but more complicated tricks can involve very large objects or even the magician appearing out of nowhere.

Rabbit from a hat

Perhaps the most famous magic trick ever performed, pulling a rabbit out of a hat, is a perfect example of production.

The rabbit is hidden under a table with a secret compartment. The hat also has a hidden opening in the top.

The hat is placed on top of the compartment so the magician can reach through it and lift the rabbit.

Magicians today might use a bunch of flowers instead of a rabbit.

Many people believe the use of live animals in magic is cruel, so this trick isn't as popular as it used to be.

John Henry Anderson.

Why it works

Like with every good trick, the audience **doesn't have all the information**. In this case, they don't know about the hidden compartment under the table, the opening in the hat, or that the rabbit was actually there all along. It will just seem like the rabbit appeared inside the hat!

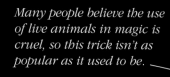

VANISHING

Vanishing is the opposite of production, where a magician's goal is to make an object or person disappear. Sometimes they are just production tricks performed in reverse, but they can also be more complicated and elaborate.

The magician Howard Thurston was known to vanish objects as big as cars in his performances.

The French Drop

Complicated hidden compartments or mirrors are often required to make big objects disappear, but magicians can vanish smaller objects using something called **sleight of hand**. One of the most famous sleight of hand techniques is the French Drop.

FACT

In 1983, the famous American magician David Copperfield made the Statue of Liberty in New York, USA, disappear in front of a live audience.

1 In one hand, hold a coin horizontally between your thumb and fingers.

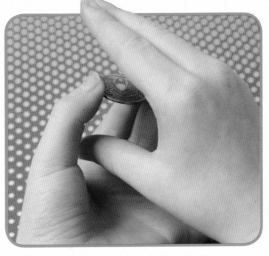

2 Reach to take it with the thumb and middle finger of your other hand.

3 Relax your grip so the coin drops past your thumb back into the original hand.

4 Close your second hand and pull it away so it looks like you take the coin with you.

5 Open your hand. It will look like the coin vanished, but it's still in the same hand.

TOP TIP

The French Drop is useful in many different tricks, and is something every magician needs to learn. It's simple to learn but hard to master, so make sure to practice it.

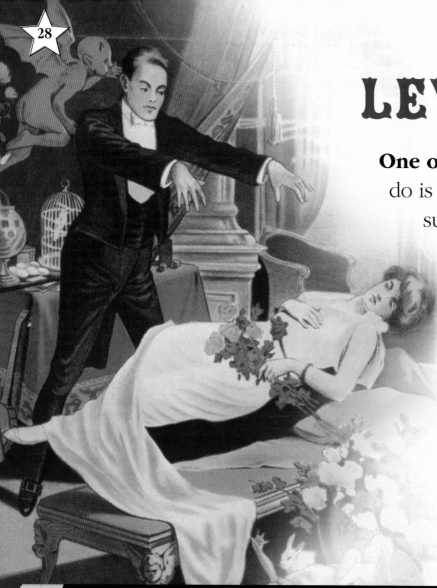

LEVITATION

One of the most amazing things a magician can do is defy gravity. Magicians use levitation and suspension to make objects or people float or appear to fly. Usually an assistant is floated, but it can also be a magician.

Levitator supreme

The American magician **Harry Kellar** was famous for a spectacular illusion where he made an assistant rise up, float across the stage, and vanish into thin air!

Kellar's famous trick "The Levitation of Princess Karna".

PREDICTION

When a magician correctly knows the outcome of an event it's called prediction. Divination is similar, but with prediction the magician must know the outcome before it has happened. Magicians use a range of clever techniques to do this.

Pick a card, any card

Prediction and divination are common in card tricks. Magicians can use sleight of hand or preparation to their advantage and "force" members of the audience to choose whichever card the magician wants them to.

The floating card

Levitation tricks can be very difficult to pull off as they often require a lot of props and preparation. Here is a fairly simple one for beginners that gives you the ability to make a card look like it's floating in thin air.

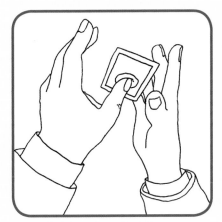 

1 Place a small piece of sticky tack on the tip of one of your thumbs. Press your thumb into the back of a card so the tack sticks to it.

2 Hold up the card between your hands as pictured. If you move your hands and fingers it will look like the card is floating.

Indian rope trick

This famous suspension is said to have been performed in India for centuries. A rope is thrown into the air – where it stays, **suspended from nothing**. A person then climbs the rope before it drops back down. However, it's widely thought that the trick is actually a fake!

"The Great Karachi" is the magician most associated with the famous trick.

Mind reading

Prediction can make it seem like a magician has the power to **read minds or see into the future**. The British magician and mentalist Derren Brown uses a combination of suggestion, misdirection, psychology, and showmanship to achieve this.

The American magician Claude Alexander was a master at mind reading tricks.

Derren Brown performs a range of amazing mental feats on both stage and television.

Crystal balls

For hundreds of years crystal balls have been used to try to make **predictions about the future**. This process is called "scrying".

ALEXANDER

THE MAN WHO KNOWS

TRANSFORMATION

When a magician's goal is to change one thing into another, the effect is called transformation. The possibilities are almost endless – it could be a card changing suit, a handkerchief that changes colour, or even an animal becoming a person!

Instant ice

This simple trick is a perfect example of transformation, and something easy to do at home. A magician pours water into a cup, then tips the cup out to reveal that the water has instantly turned into ice.

You will need
- Small sponge
- Scissors
- Paper cup
- Ice cubes
- Jug of water

1 Before you begin, place a sponge in the bottom of the cup. Make sure it fits tightly. Ask an adult to cut it down to size if necessary.

2 Place a few ice cubes on the sponge. You're now ready to start the trick at any time, but don't wait too long or the ice will melt.

3 Place the cup on a table and pour in a little water. The sponge will absorb the water and keep it trapped inside the cup.

4 Tip the cup upside down. Ice will pour out instead of water. Scrunch up the cup and throw it away.

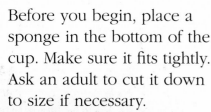

FACT

Different sponges can absorb different amounts of water. Experiment beforehand to see how much water your sponge can hold without any spilling out.

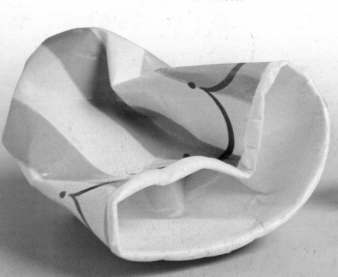

RESTORATION

Tricks involving restoration are when a magician takes a broken object – or breaks something – and returns it to its original state. For example, a rope could be cut in two and then become one piece again.

Sawing a person in half

One of the world's most famous tricks, **sawing a person in half**, is about restoration. The trick requires special equipment, perfect timing, and two assistants, and should never be attempted except by professionals.

The illusion

A magician's assistant gets inside a large box so their head and legs poke out from either end. The magician saws through the middle of the box and splits it in two. They then bring the box back together and the assistant climbs out, unharmed.

The secret

There are actually **two assistants** the entire time. Before the box is brought on stage, one of the assistants is curled up and hidden in the bottom half. When the other assistant gets in the box they curl up so they remain in the top half. At the same time, the assistant in the bottom sticks out their feet. If timed properly it will look like there is just one person in the box.

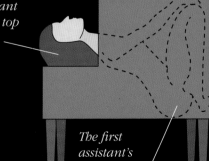

One assistant gets in the top of the box.

The first assistant's legs are never seen.

Only the second assistant's legs are ever seen.

Harry Houdini performed many death-defying escapes in public.

ESCAPOLOGY

While different from magic tricks in that the skill isn't hidden, escapology and magic are allied arts. Escapology involves a performer being placed in a set of restraints such as handcuffs, ropes, or a strait jacket. They then try to escape in a small amount of time.

Getting out!

Escape artists use various methods in their escapes. Lock picking, trick knots, hidden keys, and secret switches are all common. But it also takes **a lot of skill**, and escape artists need to be very strong, flexible, and fearless!

Strait jacket.

One of Houdini's most famous escapes was from inside this can.

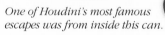

TELEPORTATION

Moving an object from one place to another in a seemingly impossible way is called teleportation. An example you may recognize is when a magician shows a card to the audience, shuffles it back into the deck, only for it to appear from somewhere else.

Making things move

Objects aren't all magicians can teleport. In one of his performances the American magician David Copperfield **teleported himself** and a member of his audience from onstage to a beach thousands of miles away.

Magicians make small objects such as coins and cards teleport with ease.

The rising card

Howard Thurston devised a very famous trick where a series of cards that an audience had chosen would magically teleport up out of the deck.

Howard Thurston called himself the "King of Cards".

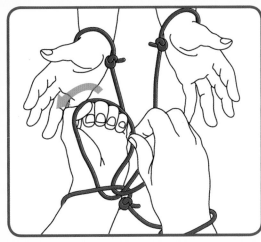

Escape from string handcuffs

It might not rival the escapes of the great Harry Houdini, but using just two pieces of string you can impress friends with this clever trick.

 Tie a loop of string around your wrists. Ask a friend to do the same to you, first crossing your string over theirs.

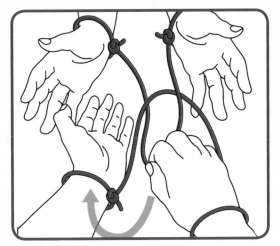

 Pull your friend's string towards you and push it through the loop on your left wrist from the back as shown.

 Bend your left hand and push it through the loop in your friend's string. Straighten out your hand.

 Pull your hands away to free yourself. Challenge your friends to see if they can figure it out.

Cups and balls

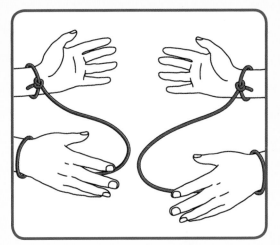

One of the most well-known teleportation tricks is cups and balls. It's also one of the earliest known tricks. **Magicians called the Acetabulari** performed shows with cups and balls in ancient Rome. Today there are many different variations of the trick, and while teleportation is the main effect, some people think of cups and balls as a mix of teleportation, vanishing, production, and transformation.

Conjurers and street performers have been doing cups and balls tricks for centuries.

FACT

When two or more objects are teleported at the same time and switch places, the effect is called "transposition".

MAKING MAGIC

This book contains more than 20 tricks for you to learn and master. The tricks are all fun, so it'll be tempting to jump right in. But before you do, there are a few things you should know.

PREPARATION

Almost all of the tricks require at least a small amount of preparation. It could involve making something, arranging a deck of cards a certain way, or writing down a prediction. But don't worry – we'll tell you exactly what you need to do. Just remember to do it before you begin.

ASSISTANCE

While most of the tricks are easy, a few of them may require an adult's help. As this adult will know the secret to the trick you won't be able to perform it for them. However, you can still practice on them – so think of them as your very own assistant!

PRACTICE

Before you try these tricks in front of an audience, you'll need to practice them first. You can do this by yourself or with an assistant, but it's very important not to skip this step. If a trick goes wrong and your audience figures out how it's done, you won't get a second chance.

DIFFICULTY

Medium

Tricks are rated between 1 and 3 stars to let you know whether they're easy, medium, or hard. But don't be put off by a hard trick – everybody is different, and some people may find certain tricks easier than others. Remember, you can always ask your assistant for help.

TOP TIP

If you're performing several tricks in a row, start with the easiest one. This will help to build up your confidence.

PATTER

Magicians love to put on a show, and you'll always hear them talking during tricks. This is known as patter, and it's a way of telling the story of the trick. Every magician has their own style of patter – some ask questions, others tell jokes – it's up to you to decide what works for you.

THE DISAPPEARING COIN

Easy

The secret to this trick is that the coin never moves – the audience will just think it has because they can't see it anymore.

This simple trick is guaranteed to amaze even the toughest audience. Nobody will be able to believe their eyes when you make a coin **VANISH** right in front of them.

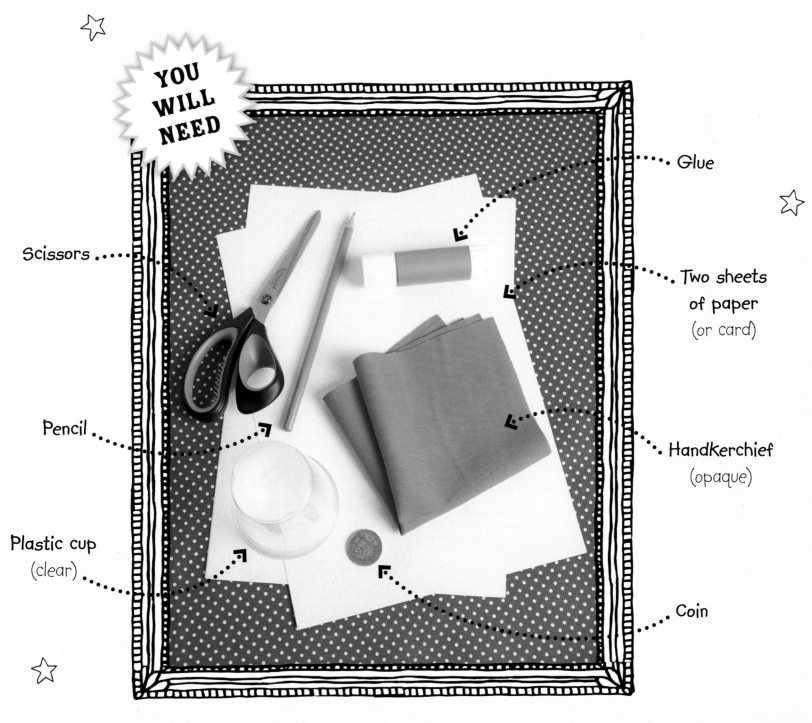

YOU WILL NEED

Scissors

Pencil

Plastic cup (clear)

Glue

Two sheets of paper (or card)

Handkerchief (opaque)

Coin

PREPARATION

1 Place the plastic cup upside down on one of the sheets of paper. Trace around the rim to create a circle, then ask an adult to cut it out.

2 Glue the circle of paper to the rim of the cup and ask an adult to trim off any excess. Discard the rest of the first sheet of paper.

3 Place the cup upside down in the middle of the second sheet of paper beside the handkerchief and the coin.

4 This is your starting point. Because the cup is on top of the paper, the audience won't be able to see the hidden circle glued to it.

PERFORMANCE

1 Place the handkerchief over the cup to cover it. Lift up the cup and handkerchief and place them on the paper over the coin.

2 Without moving the cup, lift up the handkerchief. It will look like the coin has vanished, but really it's just hidden under the paper circle.

3 To bring back the coin, put the handkerchief back over the cup and wave your hands. Lift the cup and handkerchief up and the coin will "reappear" where it had been all along.

TOP TIP

You can make this trick more impressive by asking a volunteer to supply the coin. This way they'll know it's not a trick coin. Just make sure to lay it on the paper.

THE HEAT IS ON

Have you ever wanted to convince people you have the power to read minds? This trick uses divination, which is similar to **PREDICTION**, to help you do just that!

Medium

You will need
- Variety of coins
- Small bag or pouch
- Refrigerator or freezer

PREPARATION

Place the coins in the refrigerator for about 10 minutes or the freezer for about 2 minutes to chill them. They need to be cold, but not so cold that it's obvious. When the coins are cold enough place them in the bag.

Use coins that vary in shape, size, and colour.

FACT

In a similar trick a magician has to guess which hand a volunteer holds in the air while their back is turned. Holding up your hand like that drains the blood from it, making it appear lighter. This lets the magician know which hand was held up.

PERFORMANCE

1 Tell the audience you have the power to read minds. Close your eyes and tell a volunteer to choose a coin from the bag.

2 Have your volunteer tightly hold the coin and think about a recognizable detail such as the coin's colour, shape, or the year it was made.

 3 Tell your volunteer to put the coin back in the bag and mix them up. Pour the coins on the table and touch each one, as if you're deep in thought.

4 The heat from your volunteer's hand will have warmed up the coin a little. Touch each one until you find the warm one to find their coin.

FLIGHTY COIN

Tricks don't have to be complicated to be impressive. This **TELEPORTATION** trick is an example of creating magic by doing something quicker than the eye can see.

Hard

You will need
- Coin
- Soft surface such as a tablecloth

FACT

The American magician Thomas Nelson Downs specialized in coin manipulation and caused a sensation with his act. He is sometimes referred to as the "King of Koins".

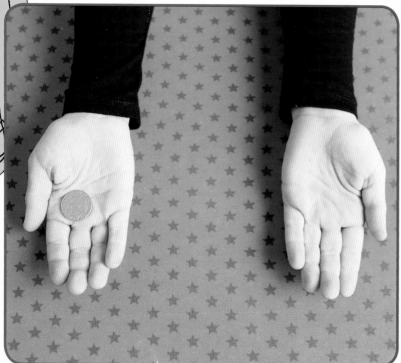

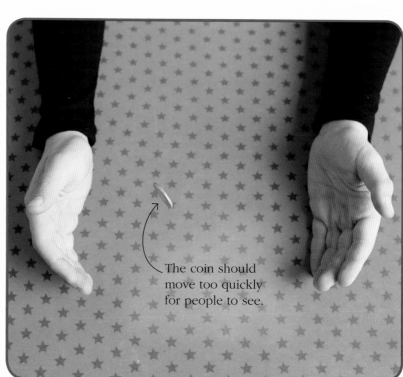

The coin should move too quickly for people to see.

1 Hold your hands face up on a soft surface. Place a coin in one of your hands near your thumb and index finger near the top of your palm.

2 Quickly turn over both of your hands so the coin flips from one hand to the other. You need to do this quickly, so it will take practice.

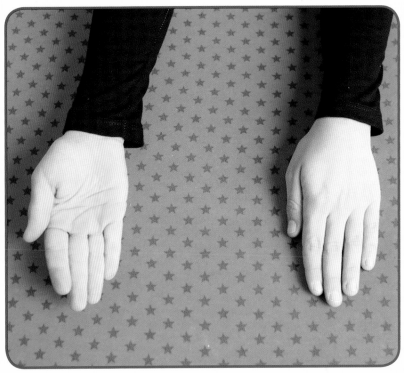

 The coin should have hit your other palm as it was turning and now be underneath it. The soft surface should have disguised any sound.

Ask someone in the audience which hand the coin was under. They will pick the original hand. Turn it over to show that the coin has vanished.

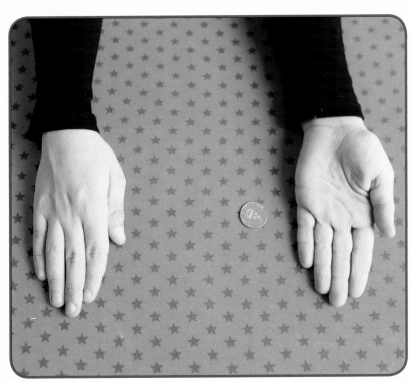

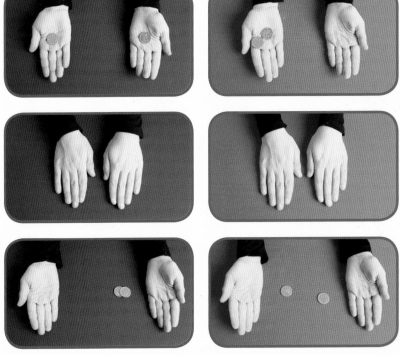

 Say something like "I wonder where it went" and turn over your other hand to reveal that the coin hadn't vanished, it had teleported!

 Once you have the technique mastered, you can use it in different ways. Try the trick with a coin in each hand or two in one hand for different results.

STACKING THE DECK

By using a clever preparation technique, magicians can force the outcome of an event. This is a key part of lots of tricks where **PREDICTION** is the desired effect.

Easy

PREPARATION

This trick isn't hard, but it requires you to set up a deck of cards so that everything works in your favour. In magic this is called "stacking the deck". For this trick you need to pick out 11 cards and place them in the following order at the top of the deck:

6, 5, 4, 3, 2, Ace, Joker, 10, 9, 8, 7

It doesn't matter which suits you use, but be sure to mix them up.

You will need
• Deck of cards

PERFORMANCE

1 Take the stacked deck and deal the top 11 cards face down in a row from left to right.

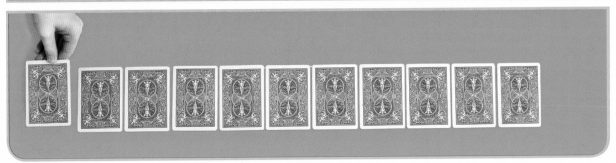

2 Turn your back and ask a volunteer to move a few cards from the right side of the row to the left (assuming they are facing opposite you). They can move as many as they want, but only one at a time. Tell them to remember how many cards they moved.

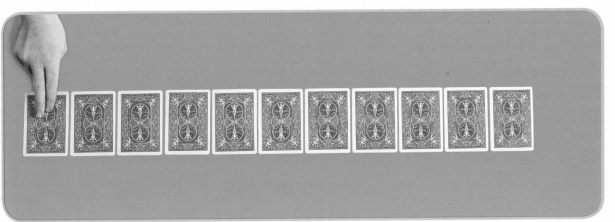

3 Turn back around and look up and down the row of cards. If you want, tap a few of the cards and look at the volunteer as if you're trying really hard to figure something out.

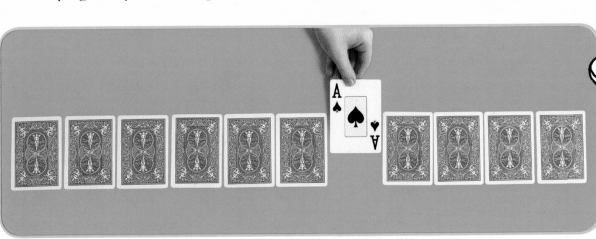

TOP TIP

Don't leave the cards out on the table before you begin. Pull the deck out of your pocket casually so the audience doesn't suspect anything.

4 Turn over the seventh card from the left. Tell the volunteer it will be the same number as the number of cards they moved. If it's an ace they moved one card, and if they didn't move any, it will be the joker.

THE MAGICIAN'S ARSENAL

There's more to magic than just learning a few basic tricks. The road to becoming a skilled magician takes a lot of time, practice, and the mastery of skills such as sleight of hand, misdirection, secrecy, and various others – all of which you'll find throughout this book.

EQUIPMENT

Magicians use lots of different tools and props in their shows. From cards and coins, to rope and rings – good magicians need to know them all.

CLOTHING

It's important for magicians to look the part while they perform their tricks. A magician's clothing look impressive, but there's more to it than meets the eye...

MISDIRECTION

In order to pull off certain tricks, magicians need to be able to distract and confuse their audience. It's often good misdirection skills that make a true master.

SLEIGHT OF HAND

Having a set of skillful actions allows magicians to do things that the audience can't see. It's an essential skill every magician needs to know.

HIDDEN SKILLS

Perhaps the most important skills a magician needs are the ones you can't see. These include patience, creativity, and confidence.

SECRECY

The ability to keep magic secrets is essential in order to protect the mystery of magic. It's not always easy to do this, but it's very important.

KEEPING SECRETS

If everybody knew how a magic trick was done, the mystery would be gone and the trick wouldn't be as interesting. A trick's secret is just as important as its execution. It's for this reason that secrecy is so important to magicians.

It can be tempting to reveal how tricks are done, but if you're ever asked how, just say, "it's magic!"

The Magician's Code

When magicians reach a certain ability level many of them will agree to help protect the mystery behind magic tricks for other people.

Magicians agree to **not give away magic secrets.** Not only would revealing how tricks work spoil things for other magicians, it can ruin it for audiences as well. Magicians also agree to only perform tricks when they have been practiced enough, and to never perform the same trick more than once for the same person.

The tale of Chung Ling Soo

The magician Chung Ling Soo took secrecy very seriously. He was born in New York as William Robinson, but spent his career **pretending to be a magician from China**. He never spoke at his shows and only a few people knew the truth.

A secret revealed

Chung Ling Soo's true identity was only discovered when a dangerous trick went wrong during one of his shows and he yelled, "Something has happened! Lower the curtain".

FACT

The Magic Circle, an organization for magicians founded in 1905, has the motto: "indocilis privata loqui", which means "not apt to disclose secrets".

MAGIC NEWSPAPER

Medium

This trick is all about the preparation. By spending the time to carefully set things up, you can create a very impressive result.

A little preparation can go a long way. The reason this **PRODUCTION** trick is so impressive to watch is that you take the time to set everything up before you begin.

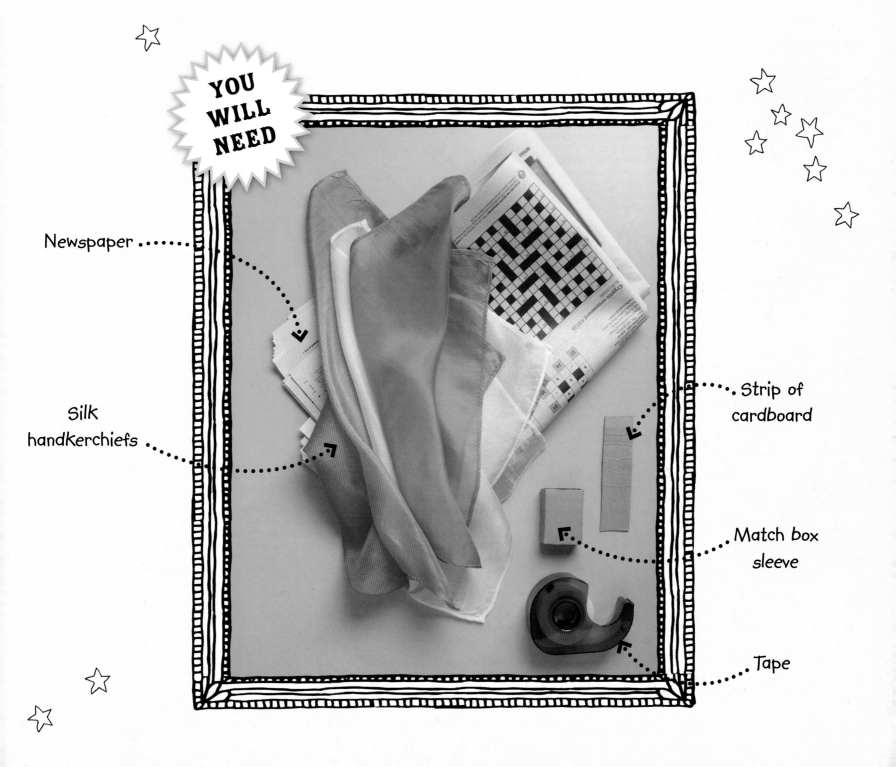

YOU WILL NEED

Newspaper

Silk handkerchiefs

Strip of cardboard

Match box sleeve

Tape

PREPARATION

 Tie a few silks or handkerchiefs together and push them into the match box sleeve. Don't worry about doing it too neatly at this stage.

Tape or glue the cardboard strip to the side of the sleeve as pictured. Make sure it's stuck on firmly so it doesn't come loose.

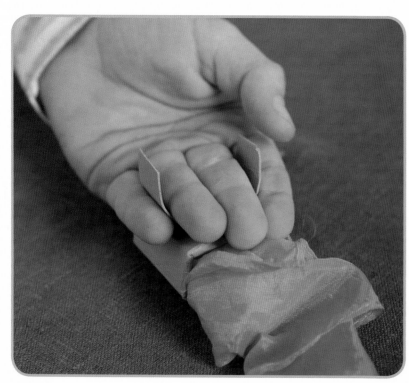

 Hold the cardboard strip between your fingers as shown. Trim off any excess but make sure you can still hold it in place comfortably.

 Push the silks all the way into the sleeve. If you've set it up properly the silks will be hidden behind your hand.

PERFORMANCE

 Stand with your body side on to the audience. Begin to flip through the pages of the newspaper, keeping the hand with the sleeve and silks hidden.

 Using your other hand, tear a little hole in the newspaper close to where your hand holding the sleeve is.

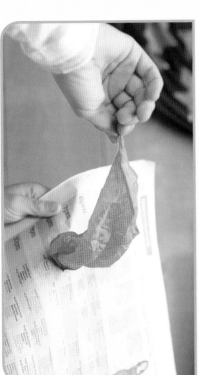

 Reach through the hole with your finger and begin to slowly pull the silks through the paper.

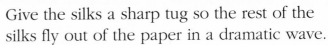

 Give the silks a sharp tug so the rest of the silks fly out of the paper in a dramatic wave.

THE RISING ACES

By preparing a deck of cards a certain way you can magically **TELEPORT** the aces. The key to the trick lies in lots of extra movements that confuse your audience.

Medium

You will need
• Deck of cards

FACT

In addition to using cards for tricks, many magicians practice the art of card throwing. Some magicians are so skilled that they can throw cards as far as 60m (196ft).

PREPARATION

Before the trick begins, find all four aces and place them face down on the top of the deck.

PERFORMANCE

1 Give the cards to a volunteer and ask them to cut the deck into four piles roughly the same size. Remember which of the piles contains the aces.

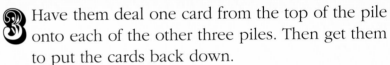

Ask the volunteer to pick up any of the piles that don't contain the aces. Tell them to move the top three cards to the bottom of the pile.

Have them deal one card from the top of the pile onto each of the other three piles. Then get them to put the cards back down.

Repeat steps 2 and 3 with the other two piles that did not contain the aces, then do the same with the final pile that does contain them.

Ask your volunteer to turn over the top card of each of the four piles, and watch their reaction when they see that all four cards are aces.

THE DISAPPEARING CUP

This trick gives you the power to make a cup **VANISH** right in front of people. All it takes is a little misdirection and for you to put on a show.

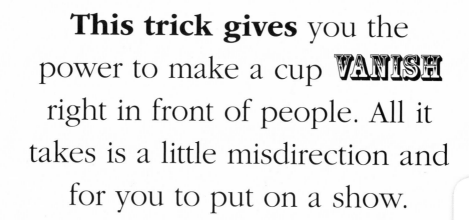

Hard

You will need
- Table and chair
- Coin
- Cup
- Paper

FACT

This trick is all about misdirection. Its success relies on the audience paying so much attention to the coin, that they don't realize it's the cup that matters.

1 Sit down and place a coin on the table. Put the cup upside down on top of it and tell the audience you can make the coin disappear.

2 Place the paper around the cup and wrap it tightly so you can see the cup's shape underneath. Wave your hands over the cup.

 3 Lift the cup and paper up. The coin will still be there, but act surprised as if the trick hasn't worked – this will distract the audience.

 4 While the audience is distracted, drop the cup into your lap. The paper will retain the shape of the cup and it will look like the cup is still there.

 5 Place the paper back down. Say something like "I wonder why that didn't work" and then wave your hands over the top of it.

 6 Squash the paper with your hands and say "Oh, it's the cup I made disappear, not the coin!" Nobody will know this was all part of the plan.

THE STICKY COIN

This quick trick involves making a coin **VANISH** from sight. Once you've got the basic technique right it's easy to pull off, making it a perfect trick for any magician.

Medium

You will need
• Double-sided tape
• Small coin

PREPARATION

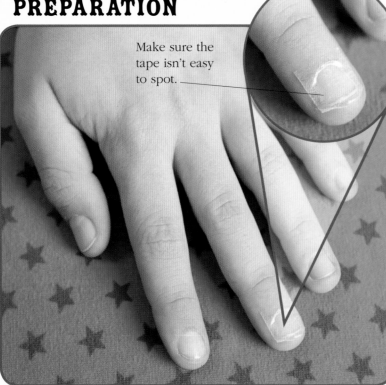

Make sure the tape isn't easy to spot.

Place a piece of double-sided tape on your middle fingernail. Practise with different amounts of tape – if it's too big the audience might see it, but if it's too small it will be hard to pick up the coin.

PERFORMANCE

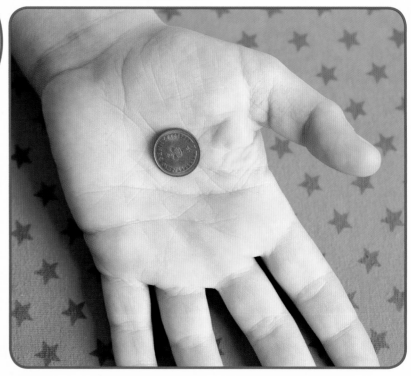

1 Hold your hands face up so that the tape is hidden. Place a coin in the bottom of the palm of the hand that has the tape on it.

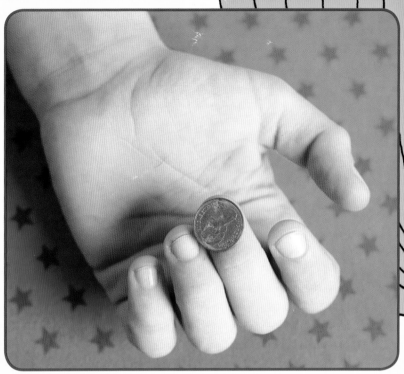

2 The next three steps need to be done as one fluid process. Firstly, close your hand into a fist and press the coin onto the tape.

3 Next, open your hand. The coin should be stuck to your fingernail. It will take a little practice to be able to do this quickly and naturally.

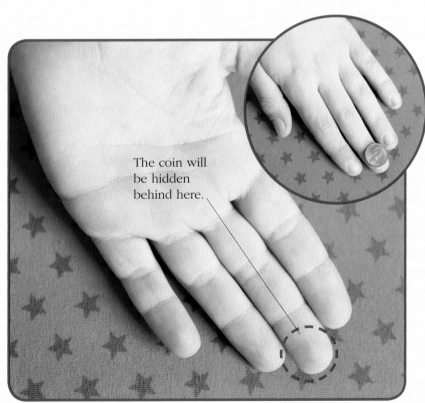

The coin will be hidden behind here.

4 Extend your fingers, keep your hand tilted downwards. If you did this quickly enough it will look like the coin vanished into thin air.

TOP TIP

This trick works best with a very small coin because it will be easier to hide behind your fingers. Small coins are also lighter, so will stick to the tape better.

THE RIGHT LOOK

A magician is a performer and showman, so looking the part is important. A magician wielding a wand while dressed in a top hat, cape, evening suit, and white gloves adds drama to a show. But a magician's clothing serves other purposes as well.

Hat

A magician's hat is an iconic **symbol of magic**. Magicians have been using them in their acts since at least the 1800s. The skillful German conjurer, Wiljada Freckel, produced flowers, a rabbit, and doves out of his hat during a show.

Magician's hats are usually black, but can be other colours too.

Magic wand

A good magician is never far from their magic wand. Not only are wands used in a variety of magic tricks, but they can also be a **powerful tool** for misdirection.

Wands are seen as an extension of the costume.

Misleading the audience

Wearing gloves can make it **hard to perform** tricks, so not every magician wears them. However, gloves can be useful in tricks. One trick involves placing a gloved hand into a hat; when it is brought out, the glove has changed colour.

Pockets and sleeves

Magicians will often use their sleeves and pockets to produce and **conceal items** using sleight of hand. For example, to help make a coin disappear, a magician might slip it up their sleeve or into a hidden pocket when the audience isn't looking.

Magicians will usually store silks in their pockets to be used in tricks.

FACT

In the early 1800s magicians used to perform in robes. It was Jean Eugène Robert-Houdin who first decided to perform in smart evening wear.

Alexander Herrmann

1844-1896

"The magician depends for the success of his art upon the credulity of the people."

Known as Herrmann the Great, Alexander Herrmann was one of the most successful and popular magicians of his day, famous for his shows throughout Europe and the Americas. He learned magic from childhood, touring with his brother Carl, first as an assistant, then as a magician in his own right. Like fellow Frenchman Jean Eugène Robert-Houdin, his particular skill was sleight of hand, but he was also famous for pulling a rabbit from a hat.

Herrmann's Beautiful Illusion —MAID OF THE MOON—

Queen of Magic

Herrmann married a young dancer called **Adelaide Scarcez** in America and they began performing together. One of their famous illusions involved Adelaide appearing to rise into the air and hover there.

Herrmann the Great & Co

The Herrmanns were sometimes called the "First Family of Magic". After Alexander died, his wife Adelaide continued performing with his **nephew Leon**. They toured together for three seasons before going their separate ways. Adelaide continued performing alone and was known as "The Queen of Magic".

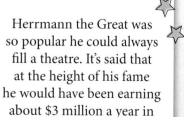

FACT

Herrmann the Great was so popular he could always fill a theatre. It's said that at the height of his fame he would have been earning about $3 million a year in today's money.

The great showman

Herrmann believed that the audience must not only be amazed by his tricks, but also amused. He was always playing **practical jokes** and on one occasion baffled two London policemen by removing their badges and planting a missing watch and handkerchief in their pockets.

COIN THROUGH A BOTTLE

Hard

The secret to this trick is to make your audience focus on the bottle. That way they'll never suspect there's a second coin.

With a little preparation and a dash of showmanship, you'll be able to pull off a classic **TELEPORTATION** trick where you move a coin through a solid bottle.

YOU WILL NEED

2 matching coins (too big to fit in bottleneck) ....

Plastic bottle (with a label)

Scissors ....

PREPARATION

1 Before you begin, peel off one end of the label. Only peel it back a little though – you don't want to remove it from the bottle.

2 Ask an adult who isn't going to watch you perform the trick to cut a small slit in the side of the bottle behind the label.

3 Push one of the coins almost all the way through the slit. You want the coin to be wedged in place without falling into the bottle.

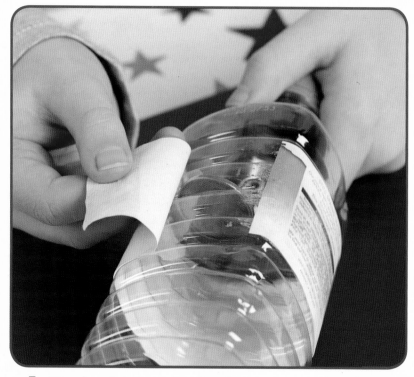

4 Neatly stick the label back down over the slit, being careful not to push the coin into the bottle. Unscrew the bottle cap and place it on the table.

PERFORMANCE

1 Hand the other coin to a volunteer to prove it's not a prop. Take it back and demonstrate that it's too big to fit through the neck of the bottle.

2 Show the audience the inside of the bottle cap to prove there's nothing inside. Screw it on to the bottle and give it a gentle tap to prove it's solid.

3 Strike the top of the bottle with the coin. The force should dislodge the hidden coin. It will happen so quickly it will look like the coin has gone through the bottle cap into the bottle.

TOP TIP

Striking the bottle will make a loud noise that distracts the audience. This is the perfect time to discreetly slip the coin in your hand into your pocket so nobody sees it and realises there were two coins all along.

TWO BECOMES ONE

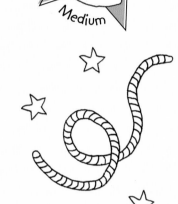

Medium

Rope tricks are often used to create the effect of **RESTORATION**. With a few clever knots you'll be able to dazzle your audience by turning two lengths of rope back into one.

You will need
• Length of rope
• Scissors

FACT

This trick is similar to the famous rope trick called cut and restore, which is a classic trick with multiple different variations.

PREPARATION

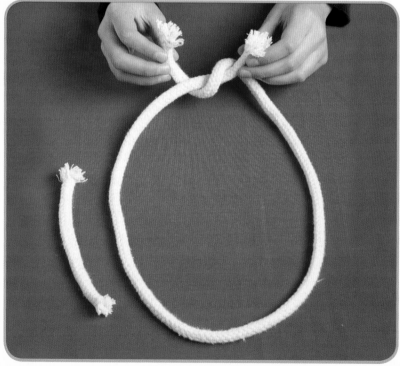

This knot makes the loop look like two pieces of rope tied together.

1 Ask an adult to cut the rope into one long length and one short length. Take both ends of the long length and tie them together to make a loop.

2 Tie the small length of rope to the loop opposite the knot you tied in step 1. It will look like the loop is made of two equal lengths of rope.

PERFORMANCE

1 Hold up the loop so the first knot you made is at the top. Tell your audience you've tied two pieces of rope together. Give the rope a tug.

2 Ask an adult to cut off the knot at the top and place it on the table. If there's no adult around, ask a friend to untie it instead.

3 Place your palm over the other knot and begin winding the rest of the rope around your other hand. Keep the knot hidden from your audience.

4 When you reach the end of the rope the knot will slide off into your palm. Keep it hidden and hold up the rope. It will have become a single piece!

CUT A PERSON IN HALF

For years magicians have used **RESTORATION** to thrill audiences by sawing a person in two and then putting them back together. Here's a version you **can** try at home!

FACT

Magicians have been sawing people in half for a long time. The English magician P.T. Selbit first performed the classic trick in 1921.

Medium

PREPARATION

If you like you can decorate the envelope.

1 Ask an adult to cut off the sides of the envelope to make a tube. It needs to be about 10cm (4in) long. Next, draw a person on a piece of paper about 4cm (1½in) wide, and about 18cm (7in) long.

2 Bend the envelope so the seam is in the middle. On one of the long sides, ask an adult to cut two slits towards the seam that are just bigger than the paper drawing. Don't cut through the seam.

PERFORMANCE

 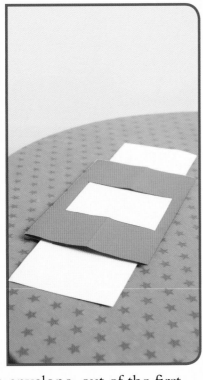 

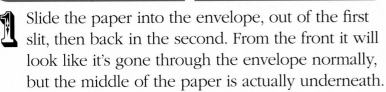 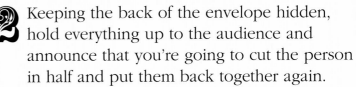

1 Slide the paper into the envelope, out of the first slit, then back in the second. From the front it will look like it's gone through the envelope normally, but the middle of the paper is actually underneath.

2 Keeping the back of the envelope hidden, hold everything up to the audience and announce that you're going to cut the person in half and put them back together again.

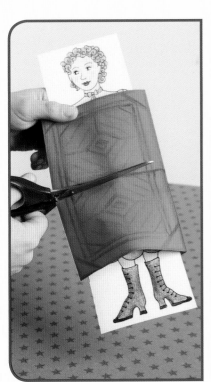  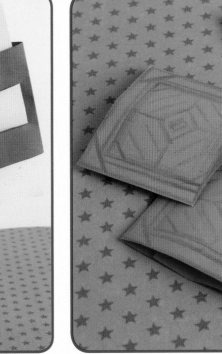 

3 Ask an adult to cut through the envelope, making sure your scissors are positioned above the middle of the paper. This way the drawing won't be cut.

4 Once you've cut all the way through, wave over the paper, pull apart the two halves of the envelope, and hold up the perfectly intact paper.

CARD PREDICTION

Medium

One of the most impressive things you can do for an audience is **PREDICT** the outcome of an event. This trick does just that in a very impressive way.

You will need
- Deck of cards
- Paper
- Pen
- Envelope
- Table

FACT
One of the reasons this trick impresses is because the volunteer believes he or she is the one touching the cards, making them think they're in control.

PREPARATION

Try to pick a card that isn't very memorable. It will seem less suspicious.

1 Before you begin, pick a card and remove it from the deck. Write or draw what the card is on the paper and seal the paper inside the envelope.

2 Place the card face down at the edge of the table so that almost half of it sticks over the side. Lay the envelope on top to hide the card.

PERFORMANCE

 Pass a deck of cards to a volunteer and tell them you're going to predict which card they will pick. Tell them to shuffle the cards to mix them all up.

 Get your volunteer to start dealing the cards face down in a rough pile. If they're doing it neatly tell them not to worry about being so careful.

When you put down the envelope the hidden card will be on top of the pile.

 Tell the volunteer to stop dealing cards whenever they like. Once they have, pick up the envelope (and hidden card) and toss it on top of the pile.

 Ask the volunteer to look at the prediction inside the envelope, then turn over the card at the top of the pile. Your prediction was right!

MAGIC WANDS

Wands aren't just for magicians. Throughout history they have been used in one form or another by wizards, druids, alchemists, Greek and Egyptian gods, and witches.

Sorcerers and wizards in ancient times convinced people that their wands were a source of great magical power. This is no longer the case, and the modern magic wand serves as more of a prop, but it will always be seen as a symbol of magic.

Historical wands

Wands have appeared in various shapes and sizes in many cultures as staves or rods, king's sceptres, shaman's drumming sticks, wizard's staffs, and even a conductor's baton. Wands have been made from many **different materials** such as wood, ivory, stone, and even gold and silver. Some wands were carved with symbolic images for use in rituals.

Harry Blackstone

One of Harry Blackstone Sr's famous props was an **oversized magic wand**. It looked just like the classic black and white wand most magicians use, but was 86cm (34in) long!

Shaman's drumming stick   *Magician's wand*   *African staff*   *Chinese sceptre*

A magician's tool

Wands are tools of the trade that magicians use to convince the audience that something magical has occurred. Wands can also be used for **misdirection** – if a magician is spinning his wand, the audience's attention will be focused on the wand rather than on the magician's secret actions.

FACT

When a magician dies, a broken wand ceremony is sometimes performed at their funeral. A wand is broken as a symbol that their death has caused the wand to lose its magic.

Howard Thurston
1869-1936

"My object is to mystify and entertain. I wouldn't deceive you for the world."

One of the great American magicians, Thurston created the largest travelling magic show in the world. His entourage of costumes, props, and equipment needed eight train cars to carry it. He was a very skilled card magician, but he also performed a variety of spectacular illusions such as making a white horse and rider vanish into thin air, topped only by the sports car and passengers that mysteriously disappeared.

During Easter celebrations at the White House, Thurston produces an egg from the mouth of President Roosevelt's grandson.

FACT

Thurston's "Magic Box of Candy" was a set of simple magic tricks for beginners. Around 2 million were sold in total, but many magicians frowned upon revealing secrets to even the simplest tricks.

Hat trick

Thurston started out as a skilful **card manipulator**, but was determined to master other areas of magic. Through creative use of props, Thurston developed illusions that were highly entertaining, including drawing all manner of objects such as scarves, flags, and rabbits from a hat.

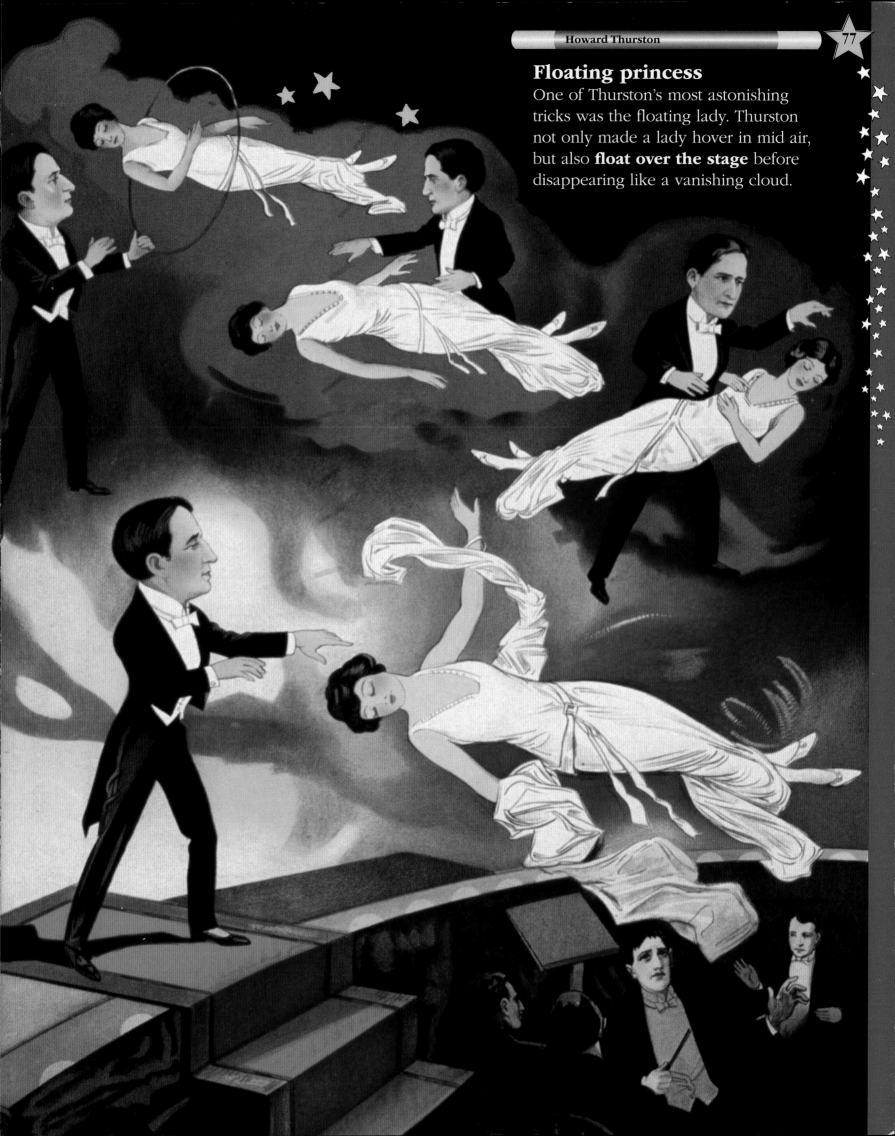

Floating princess

One of Thurston's most astonishing tricks was the floating lady. Thurston not only made a lady hover in mid air, but also **float over the stage** before disappearing like a vanishing cloud.

SLEIGHT OF HAND

One of the most important tools a magician has is sleight of hand. Sleight of hand is a set of special techniques that are used to help pull off tricks. It's so important that you could say that without sleight of hand, magic as we know it simply couldn't exist.

What is sleight of hand?

Sleight of hand is the act of doing something the **audience doesn't see**. This can be many things, but common sleights include hiding objects, moving objects to a new place, and swapping an object for a different one.

SLEIGHT OF HAND TIPS

1. Talking to the audience to misdirect them will break their concentration. This is the perfect time to perform a sleight of hand action.

2. If you look at your hands while you perform a trick, so will the audience. So be careful not to do this unless that's where you want them to look.

3. Practising tricks in front of a mirror will help you see what your audience sees. This will let you know if your technique needs changing.

FACT

Sleight of hand is also known by the term "prestidigitation", which means "nimble fingers".

Seven principles of sleight of hand

The magical duo Penn and Teller came up with this list of sleight of hand techniques. Don't worry if it seems hard at first, even experts take years perfecting sleight of hand. The important thing to remember is the audience must not see what's you're doing.

Palm – Secretly holding an object in a hand that seems empty.

Ditch – Getting rid of an object without anybody noticing.

Steal – Secretly getting an object you need.

Load – Moving an object to a certain place.

Simulation – Making it look like something has happened when it hasn't.

Misdirection – Directing the audience's attention away from the sleight.

Switch – Swapping one object for another one without anyone knowing.

Quicker than the eye

Sleight of hand is achieved using a combination of quick, fluid hand movements and taking advantage of angles and blind spots in the audience's vision. The key is trying to **trick the audience's senses**

MAGIC SOCIETIES

Over the years, magicians have set up private clubs to further the study of magic. Some of these groups are secret, while others are known to the public. At these clubs the magicians share tricks, chat about their trade, and swap stories. Only magicians are allowed to join these organizations.

FACT

In order to maintain the mystery of magic, magicians agree not to reveal magical secrets before being allowed into many of these clubs.

The Magic Circle
This club was founded in London in 1905. Members promise never to discuss secrets with anyone who is not a magician. The club's home has a theatre, museum, and Club Room.

International Brotherhood of Magicians
Based in Missouri, USA, the IBM has more than 10,000 members in 80 countries. It includes professionals and amateurs, including children as young as 7 years old. It publishes a monthly magazine for its members.

Society of American Magicians
This is the oldest organization for stage magicians in the world. It is based in California and has about 30,000 members. It publishes a magazine and there is also a youth organization for members under 18.

London Society of Magicians
The LSM was founded in a pub in London in 1941 for magicians who visited during World War II. After the war the group continued to meet. They share ideas, hold competitions, and raise money for charity.

Magic societies help to further the practice of magic in several ways. One of these is providing guidance to young magicians.

TEACHING

To preserve the art of magic, many societies set up special mentoring programs so that young magicians can learn from the best in the business.

SOCIAL

Not everything has to be about magic! Societies can simply be a great place for magicians to meet and get to know people who have similar interests to their own.

HISTORY

Preserving the history of magic is one of the most important roles these organizations play. Many of them have museums filled with important documents and items.

PERFORMING

Many of the world's best magicians belong to exclusive clubs. One of the benefits of joining is being able to enjoy private performances from their friends and rivals.

THE GHOST TUBE

Medium

The success of this great trick hinges on building a secret compartment to store the items you want to make appear.

Is it impossible to make objects appear from thin air? This clever **PRODUCTION** trick will help you to prove otherwise in a very memorable way!

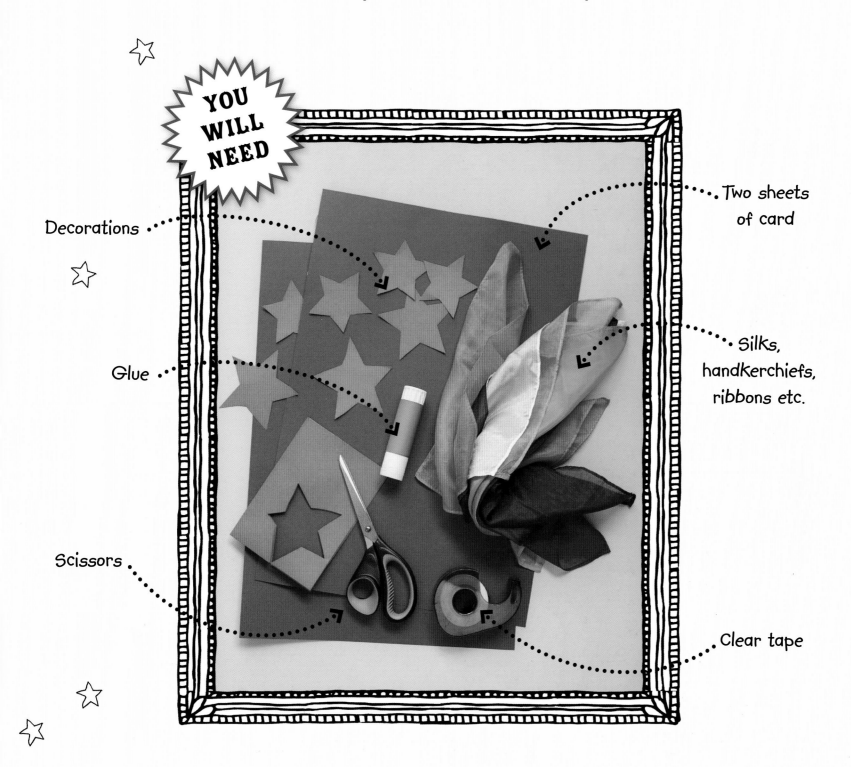

YOU WILL NEED

Two sheets of card

Silks, handkerchiefs, ribbons etc.

Clear tape

Decorations

Glue

Scissors

PREPARATION

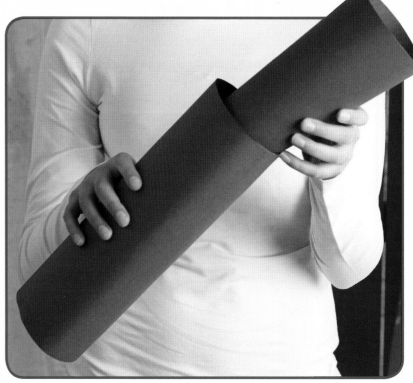

1. Roll one sheet of card into a tube-like cylinder and secure it with tape. Roll the other sheet into a cone so one end is a little narrower than the other.

2. Put the cone inside the cylinder so the thick ends line up. Tape it in place and trim off any excess. If you want, glue on stars to decorate it.

3. When it's finished, one side should look like a normal tube and the other should have a small gap created by the cone.

4. Fill the hidden gap with whatever you are going to pull out of it. Use small items that don't take up too much space such as silks or handkerchiefs.

PERFORMANCE

1 Show the audience the end of the tube that looks normal. Keep the end with the hidden gap pointing away from them at all times.

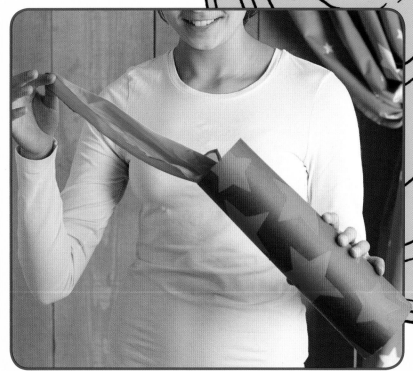

2 Drop a coin through the tube to prove that it's hollow and there are no mirrors, then pull out one of the hidden items from the gap.

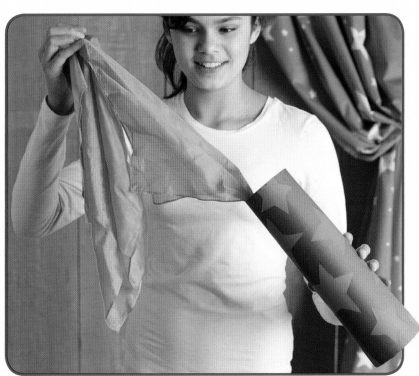

3 As the audience watches in amazement, continue to pull things out of the tube. Repeat this until it's empty and give the tube a shake.

TOP TIP

Make sure nobody ever sees the other end of the tube or the trick will be spoiled. A good tip is to hold the tube vertically when you pull objects out.

CUPS AND BALLS

This classic trick combining **TELEPORTATION**, **PRODUCTION**, and **VANISHING** may date back as far as ancient Egypt! It's no wonder it still amazes audiences today.

Hard

You will need
- 3 cups
- 4 small balls

PREPARATION

Line up three balls on a table and place a cup by each one. Hide a secret fourth ball in the middle cup. It's important that the audience never knows the fourth ball exists.

PERFORMANCE

1 Turn over one of the outer cups and place it down behind the ball and then turn over the other outer cup with your other hand.

2 Turn over the middle cup, making sure that the hidden ball doesn't fall out. Try to make it look the same as when you turned over the other cups.

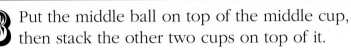

3 Put the middle ball on top of the middle cup, then stack the other two cups on top of it.

4 Tap the stack of cups, then lift it up and say "look, the ball has moved through the bottom of the cup!"

5 Flip the cups right side up. Then line them up like in step 2, with the middle cup over the middle ball. Put one of outer balls on the middle cup and stack the other cups on top of it like in step 3.

6 Tap and lift the cups again. This time there will be two balls underneath. This is because the middle cup contained the extra ball from earlier.

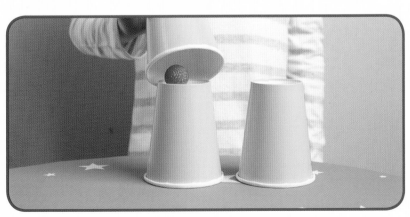

7 Repeat the stacking process again with the final ball, being careful not to let the extra ball fall out when you put the middle cup over the two balls.

8 Lift the stack of cups up again to reveal that the final ball has joined the others underneath the cups. Your audience won't believe their eyes!

MULTIPLY MONEY

This trick uses the effect of **TRANSFORMATION** to turn one coin into two others in a flash. It's easy to learn, but hard to pull off like a master.

Hard

You will need
- 1 small coin
- 2 larger coins

FACT

This trick is an example of how magicians only let the audience see what they want them to see in order to pull off a trick.

PREPARATION

1 Hold the two large coins horizontally between your thumb and index finger.

2 Position the smaller coin vertically in front of the bigger coins to hide them from view.

PERFORMANCE

 Show your audience the coin, but hold it so that they can't see the other ones behind it. The next steps need to be done in one quick motion.

Bring your hands together and use your thumb to slide the smaller coin over the others to make a stack.

The big coin will obscure the small one.

Split the stack in two, taking one coin in one hand, and two in the other. One of the big coins will hide the small one from view.

Lift your hands up to the audience. If you did this quickly it'll look like the small coin split into two and changed entirely.

THE MAGIC STRING

Do you think it's possible to magically repair a piece of string? By using the power of **RESTORATION** you will be able to make it seem like it is.

Medium

PREPARATION

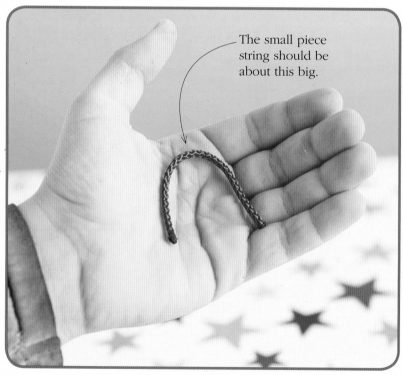

The small piece string should be about this big.

Take the small length of string, about 5cm (2in) should be about the right size, and hide it in the palm of your left hand as pictured.

PERFORMANCE

1 Hold up the long length of string in your other hand to prove to the audience that it's just one single length.

2 Take the long length of string into your left hand as shown, but push the hidden loop of string above it so it sticks out of the top of your hand.

3 Ask an adult in the audience to cut the string into two pieces by cutting through the loop that's sticking out of your hand.

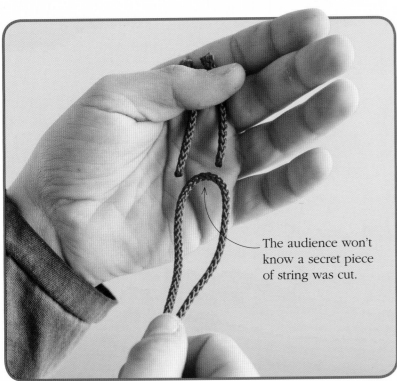

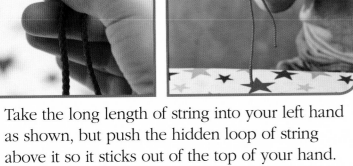

The audience won't know a secret piece of string was cut.

4 Secretly tuck the ends of the short string into your hand. Hold them in place with your thumb and pull the long string out with a dramatic wave.

5 Hold the string up to the audience. It will seem as if the piece that was cut has magically repaired and become whole again!

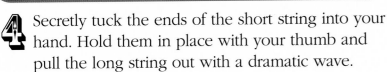

TOOLS OF THE TRADE

It doesn't matter what tools magicians use to dazzle their audience – the best performers can make magic from almost anything. However, there are a few pieces of equipment that all magicians should have in their box of tricks.

Silks

These colourful handkerchiefs are small enough to be scrunched up and **hidden in various places**. Magicians use silks for tricks that involve production, as pulling them out of the air looks dramatic.

Cups and balls

A favourite of **street performers**, magicians have been dazzling audiences with various cups and balls routines for years.

A DECK OF CARDS

A standard deck of cards contains 52 playing cards that divides into **four suits**: diamonds, hearts, clubs, and spades. Each suit is made up of 9 numbered cards, a jack, queen, king, and an ace.

Rope

In addition to being used by **escape artists**, rope is used for many magic tricks. Rope tricks usually involve changing a rope's length, joining pieces of rope together, or cutting a length of rope into pieces and making it whole again.

FACT

A lot of more advanced magic tricks require special equipment such as trick card decks, coins that bend in half, and boxes with secret compartments.

Cards

Playing cards are probably the most famous tool that a magician has at their disposal. Magicians love them because they're **small enough to manipulate**, but also have lots of different uses.

Linking rings

A stage magic classic, linking rings are a number of metal hoops that pass through each other and link up to **create chains**. Magicians have been performing tricks with linking rings for hundreds of years.

Coins

A favourite tool of sleight of hand experts, coins can be used for many amazing tricks. However, a lot of coin tricks can be very difficult, and so take a **lot of practice** to master.

Harry Houdini
1874-1926

"What the eyes see and the ears hear, the mind believes."

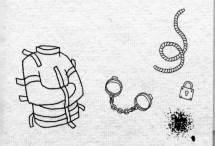

Harry Houdini was the world's greatest escape artist. He escaped from locked rooms, padlocked chests, handcuffs, and other traps with ease. Houdini used clever publicity stunts to raise his profile, and he became one of the most famous and highly paid stage stars of the early 20th century. Houdini kept how he managed to escape from secure locks a secret, and to this day nobody is really certain how he performed some of his escapes.

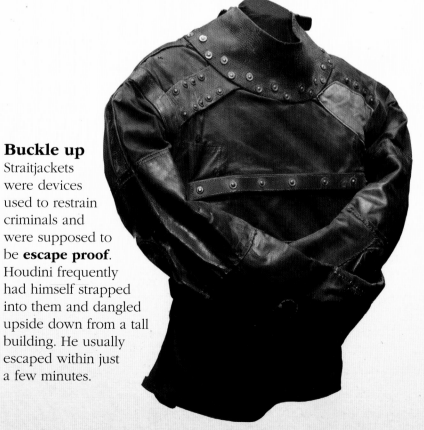

Buckle up
Straitjackets were devices used to restrain criminals and were supposed to be **escape proof**. Houdini frequently had himself strapped into them and dangled upside down from a tall building. He usually escaped within just a few minutes.

Manacled man
When Houdini arrived in a new town he sometimes publicly challenged the police to lock him up. As newspaper reporters watched, Houdini would escape from handcuffs, manacles, or even prison cells. This would assure him huge publicity for his stage show and tickets would sell in large numbers.

Escape from East River

In July 1912, Houdini performed one of his most famous escapes. He was locked in handcuffs and leg irons, which were nailed to the inside of a wooden crate. He was then locked inside the crate and **thrown into the East River** in New York City. The crate sank, but 57 seconds later Houdini swam free. The crate was pulled up and found to be still locked shut with the restraints still inside.

The Houdinis

Houdini always worked with a partner. At first he worked with his brother Dash and used the name "The Brothers Houdini", and after he married Bess Rahner in 1894 they performed as **"The Houdinis"**. It is thought his assistant would distract the audience while Houdini was doing his tricks.

BURIED ALIVE!
EGYPTIAN FAKIRS OUTDONE

Master Mystifier
HOUDINI
THE GREATEST NECROMANCER OF THE AGE—PERHAPS OF ALL TIMES
The Literary Digest

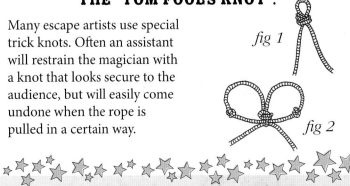

TRICKS OF THE TRADE

THE "TOM FOOL'S KNOT".

Many escape artists use special trick knots. Often an assistant will restrain the magician with a knot that looks secure to the audience, but will easily come undone when the rope is pulled in a certain way.

fig 1

fig 2

THE TIGHTROPE BALL

Medium

The secret to this trick is that the audience can't see there's a hidden piece of thread that keeps the ball from falling.

One of the most impressive feats in magic is making things float or LEVITATE. This trick lets you suspend a ball in the air with nothing but a steady hand and a little preparation.

YOU WILL NEED

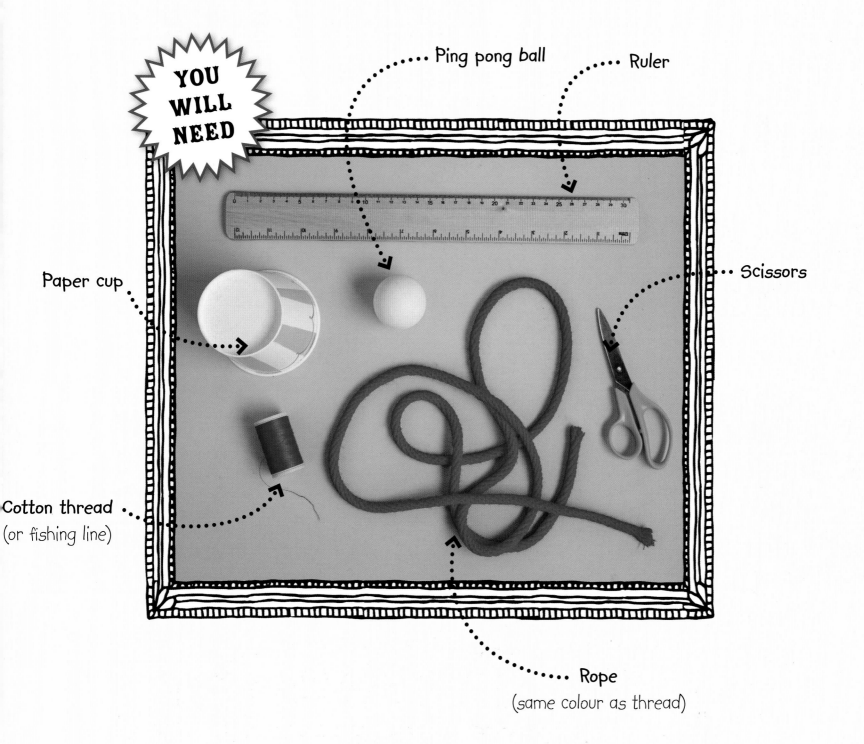

Ping pong *ball*

Ruler

Paper cup

Scissors

Cotton thread
(or fishing line)

Rope
(same colour as thread)

PREPARATION

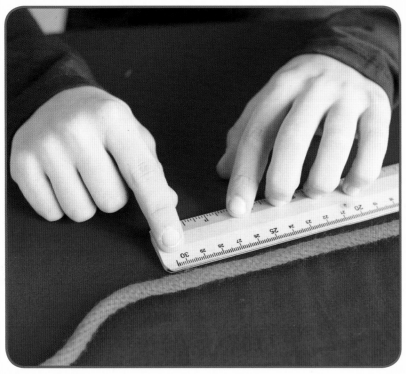

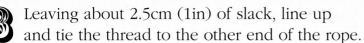 Lay the rope straight and measure out a 30cm (12in) length. Ask an adult to cut it with scissors.

Tightly tie the cotton thread near one of the ends of the rope. Ask an adult to cut off any excess.

The audience shouldn't be able to see the thread.

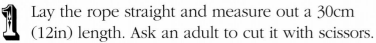 Leaving about 2.5cm (1in) of slack, line up and tie the thread to the other end of the rope.

When you perform the trick, you need to separate the rope and thread with your fingers as shown.

PERFORMANCE

1 Place the paper cup upside down on the table and position the ping pong ball on top.

2 Holding the rope and thread as instructed earlier, lower them over the ball so they sit on either side.

3 Separate your hands so the rope and thread go taut. Lift your hands and the ball will raise too.

4 For a bit of added flair, gently tilt the rope and thread so the ball rolls up and down along it.

AN IMPOSSIBLE PREDICTION

Medium

It's very common for card tricks to be based around **PREDICTION** or divination. The reason for this is that there are so many ways to use cards to achieve this effect.

You will need
- Cards
- Pen
- Paper

FACT

The Austrian magician Johann Nepomuk Hofzinser is considered by many to be the father of card magic. Many of the techniques he invented in the early 1800s are still used by magicians today.

PREPARATION

Before you begin, pick a card and put it at the top of the deck. Write or draw what the card is on a piece of paper, and hide the paper somewhere.

PERFORMANCE

1 Take the deck of cards in one hand and slide the top card into your other hand. As you do this, tell the audience you want them to pick a card.

2 Holding the card in place with your fingers, spread the rest of the deck on top. Tell a volunteer to say "stop" when they've chosen a card.

3 When the volunteer says stop, split the deck in two. As you do, secretly slide the hidden card to the bottom of where you cut the deck.

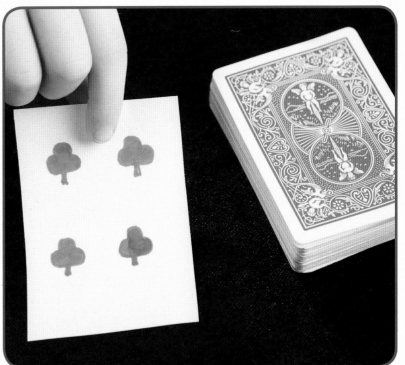

4 Hold the deck up to the audience. If you did it properly, the hidden card will be the card at the bottom instead of the one they picked.

5 Ask the volunteer to read their chosen card aloud. Once they have, direct them to the paper you hid earlier. Your prediction will match their card.

MYSTERY COLOUR

Easy

This trick is as simple as it is effective. Not even the most clever audience will be able to figure out how you correctly **DIVINE** which colour their crayon is.

You will need
- Crayons
- Small bag or pouch

FACT

The British mentalist Derren Brown, famous for impressive feats, once performed a stunt where he "predicted" all of the numbers in a lottery.

1 Place a selection of different coloured crayons into a small bag and give it to a volunteer.

2 Turn around. With your hands behind your back, ask the volunteer to place a crayon in your palm.

The crayon will leave a mark under your nail.

 Turn back around and tell your volunteer you're going to guess what colour the crayon is. As you do, scrape the crayon with your thumbnail.

4 Ask the volunteer to put the crayon back in the bag and hand it back to you. Hold it up in front of you and pretend that you're thinking hard.

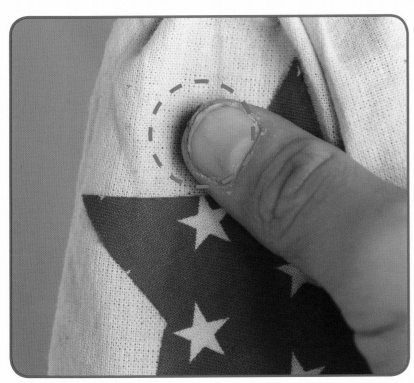

 Secretly take a glance at your thumb. Nobody will know how, but you'll be able to tell what colour the crayon was by looking at your nail.

TOP TIP

When you look at your thumb try not to give away what you're doing. One idea is to pretend you're trying to look "through" the bag.

THE CHANGING CARD

This trick can be a little hard to get right at first, but being able to make a card magically **TRANSFORM** into another is one of the most amazing tricks a beginner can learn.

Hard

You will need
• Deck of cards

WHAT THE AUDIENCE SEES

1 This trick, invented by S.W. Erdnase, is a little different to the others. You'll need to know exactly what the audience is meant to see in order to be able to do it properly.

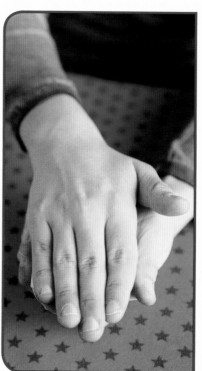

2 The audience should see you slide your hand over a card, only for it to change into a different one when you pull your hand away.

HOW TO DO IT

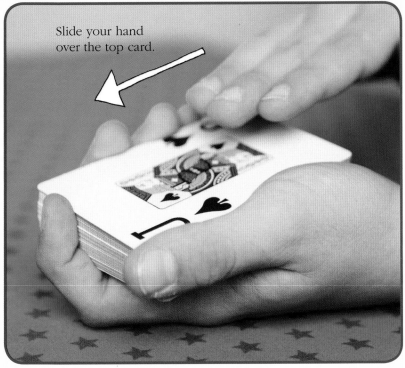

Slide your hand over the top card.

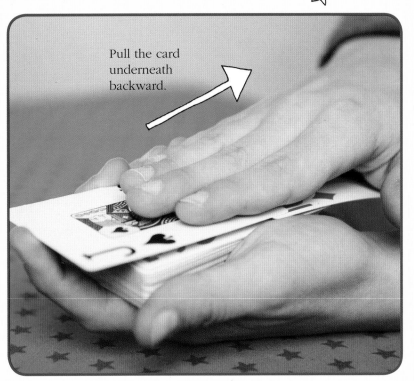

Pull the card underneath backward.

 Prepare a deck so the two cards at the bottom are different colours. Turn the deck face up and slide your hand over it. As you do, push the top card forward using the top part of your palm.

 Moving the card forward will expose the second card a little. Next, slide your hand back and use the bottom of your palm to slide it all the way out from underneath the first card.

Try to keep the cards covered with your hand.

 Slide the second card forwards so it moves on top of the original card. Try to keep the cards hidden by your hand at all times. Then use your hands to even out the deck so it looks neat.

 The card on top will have changed! It may take a while before you can do this whole sequence in one motion. If that's the case, practice each step individually until you can put it all together.

Harry August Jansen

1883-1955

"Sim Sala Bim".

These magic words were the mark of the magician known as "Dante". Nonsense words taken from a Danish nursery rhyme – they set the mood for the magic to come, and Dante knew how to create a stage impression. His shows included as many as forty performers, with musicians, jugglers and acrobats, birds and animals, as well as Dante's amazing tricks and illusions.

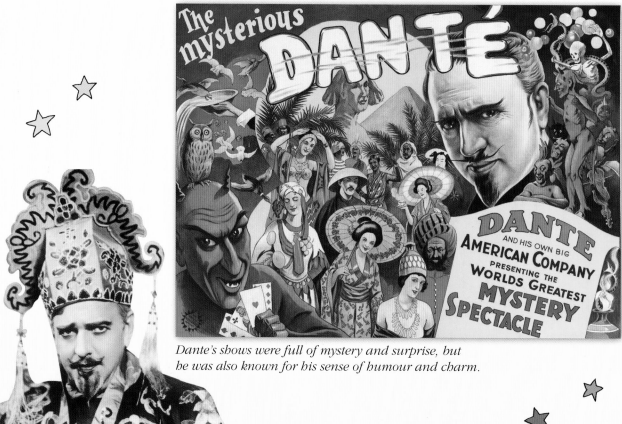

Dante's shows were full of mystery and surprise, but he was also known for his sense of humour and charm.

International master

Dante took his family with him when travelling the world. His wife had been a musician and led a 40-piece orchestra and his children were comfortable with audiences in Africa, India, China, and Japan.

Stage success

Dante's manager claimed he was the world's greatest stage artist. He presented a show in **seven languages** and appeared before Kings and Presidents in Sweden, Norway, Denmark, Greece, and Russia.

FACT

Dante was such an important magician, that after he died in 1955 many magicians said that the "Golden Age of Magic" had come to an end.

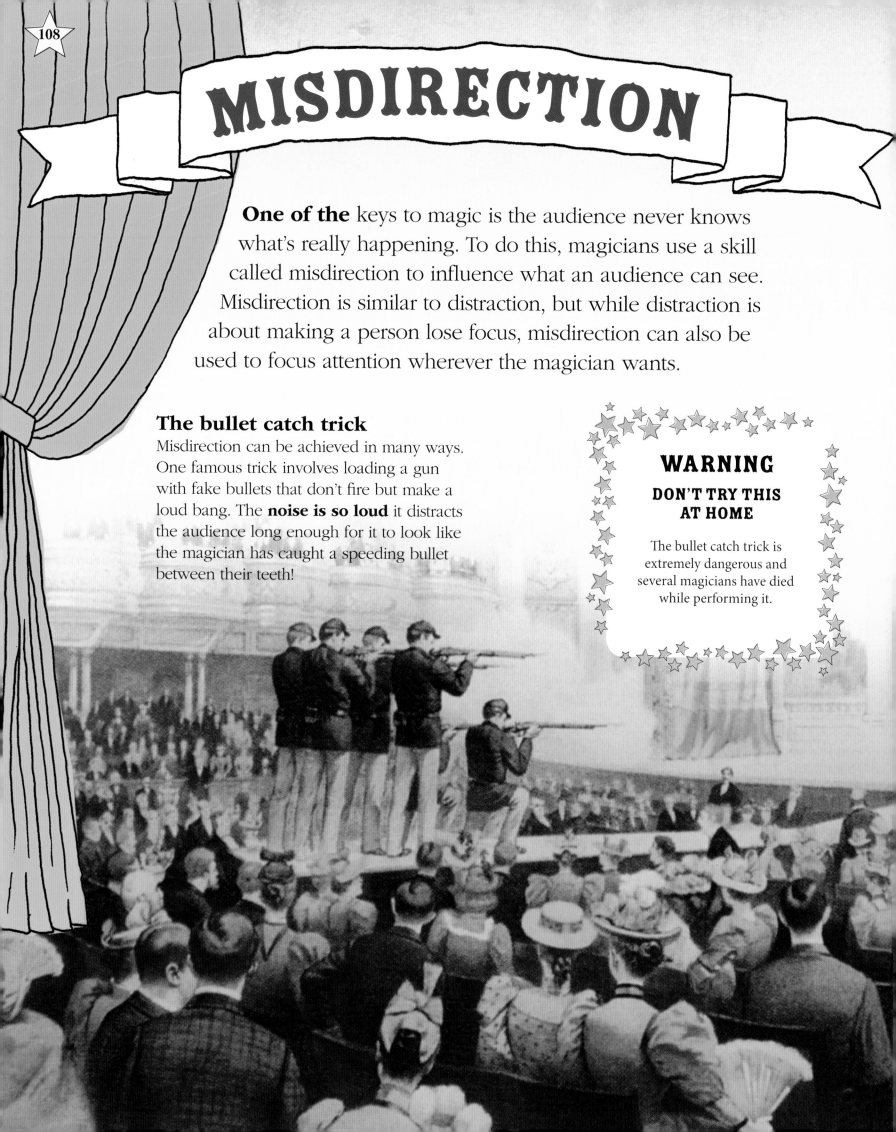

MISDIRECTION

One of the keys to magic is the audience never knows what's really happening. To do this, magicians use a skill called misdirection to influence what an audience can see. Misdirection is similar to distraction, but while distraction is about making a person lose focus, misdirection can also be used to focus attention wherever the magician wants.

The bullet catch trick

Misdirection can be achieved in many ways. One famous trick involves loading a gun with fake bullets that don't fire but make a loud bang. The **noise is so loud** it distracts the audience long enough for it to look like the magician has caught a speeding bullet between their teeth!

WARNING
DON'T TRY THIS AT HOME

The bullet catch trick is extremely dangerous and several magicians have died while performing it.

FACT

The human brain is drawn to movement and bright colours. This is why when a magician waves a magic wand or silk handkerchief, the audience will naturally look that way.

PHYSICAL

The most common misdirection involves a magician pretending to do one thing with their hands while they are actually doing something else. This can be anything from pretending to pick up an object or moving their hands in a certain way, but it's very important that it looks natural.

While the audience is distracted by the noise, the magician quickly moves the bullet between his teeth.

MENTAL

It's natural for audiences to want to know the secret to a trick, so skilled magicians use this to their advantage and sometimes let the audience think they have figured out the secret. Doing this will lower the audience's guard, allowing the magician to do whatever it is they wanted.

VERBAL

Most magicians talk during their shows to make them more entertaining – but talking during tricks has another purpose. When an audience is distracted by what the magician is saying, it will be harder to spot whatever it is that the magician is doing.

STREET MAGIC

Street magic stretches back as far back as the days of ancient Rome, and has existed in various forms such as circuses, busking, side shows, and fairs ever since. Today street magic is undergoing a big revival led by a new wave of magicians who require a bigger arena and audience for their illusions.

Art and magic

Magic has fascinated artists for years. In the 15th century the Dutch artist **Hieronymus Bosch** painted "The Conjurer", showing a street magician performing with cups and balls and producing a frog from a man's mouth.

Cool trickery

The British magician Dynamo (Steven Frayne) is a new breed of magician who **doesn't rely on big stage sets**. His street illusions include levitating with one hand on a moving bus, walking on water, and appearing to pass through a solid glass window.

Jeff Sheridan is also a renowned magic inventor and visual artist.

Father of Modern Street Magic

Jeff Sheridan is a famous magician who started his career **establishing modern street magic** and making it respectable with dazzling performances in New York City's Central Park. Sheridan went on to a career in Europe including as house artist of the leading variety theatre in Germany, the Tigerpalast of Frankfurt. He has influenced many important magicians, including David Copperfield, David Blaine and Jeff McBride.

The ultimate in street magic?

David Blaine's most famous stunts are all **performed on the streets**. These include hanging over London in a locked box for 44 days, being encased in ice, being buried alive for a week, and holding his breath for 17 minutes. His most electrifying stunt was being surrounded by deadly electric currents.

Blaine stood in the currents for three days!

The currents contained a million volts of electricity.

FACT

Audiences love street magic because they know the magician doesn't have access to the props they would on a stage, and are therefore using nothing but pure skill to pull off amazing tricks.

TRUTH OR TRICKERY?

While many of the tricks performed by magicians and escape artists can be dangerous, there are other types of performers who use their bodies in unique ways to create a range of spectacular and dangerous feats. While none of these acts are magical illusions, the audience may wrongly believe there is trickery at work.

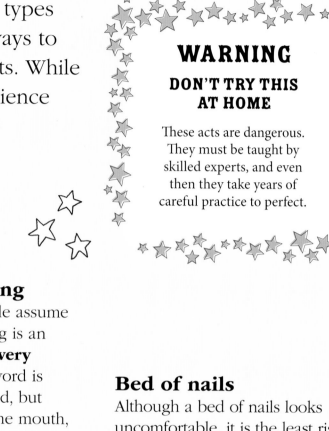

WARNING
DON'T TRY THIS AT HOME

These acts are dangerous. They must be taught by skilled experts, and even then they take years of careful practice to perfect.

Sword swallowing
Although many people assume that sword swallowing is an illusion, it is actually **very rarely faked**. The sword is not actually swallowed, but it is passed through the mouth, down the throat towards the stomach. The sword isn't very sharp, but performers can still badly injure themselves if they're not very careful.

Bed of nails
Although a bed of nails looks uncomfortable, it is the least risky of these feats. If there are enough nails for the person's **weight to be spread evenly** the nails will not break the skin. Getting on and off the nails is the hardest part, as the weight of the person is supported by just a few nails.

Fire eating

Traditionally performed at festivals or as street art, fire eating is the act of extinguishing a flaming object by putting it into the mouth to **cut off the oxygen supply** to the flame. Fire eating looks spectacular but the performer often has to endure pain caused by blisters on the tongue, throat, and on the lips.

Fire breathing

Dating back to ancient Egypt, fire breathers blow fuel onto a flame so it looks like they are **shooting flames** out of their mouth. By using different techniques, they can produce a dramatic fireball, a huge blast upwards, or direct flames downwards, sending the fire blast to the ground.

HISTORY OF MAGIC

Magic has changed a lot over the years. Its journey has spanned continents and thousands of years. But what's next? And what tricks might the future have in store?

c.25,000BCE
The cave at Altamira in Spain is decorated with paintings of bison, deer, and other animals, perhaps as part of a magic ritual.

c.1600BCE
Egyptian priests collect together a number of magical spells to form the *Book of the Dead*, intended to help people pass into the next life.

c.720
Birth of the alchemist Jabir ibn Hayyan, also famous as a geographer, philosopher and physicist.

2000BCE — **0CE** — **1000**

c.2000BCE
The I Ching system of divination begins to be used in China.

c.300BCE
I Ching becomes its modern form in China.

c.50CE
The cups and balls routine is performed in ancient Rome using stones and pots.

c.1500BCE
The Eleusinian Mysteries begin to be celebrated in honour of the goddess Demeter.

924
King Athlestan passes a law against witchcraft in England, making the act of witchcraft punishable by a fine of 120 shillings or death.

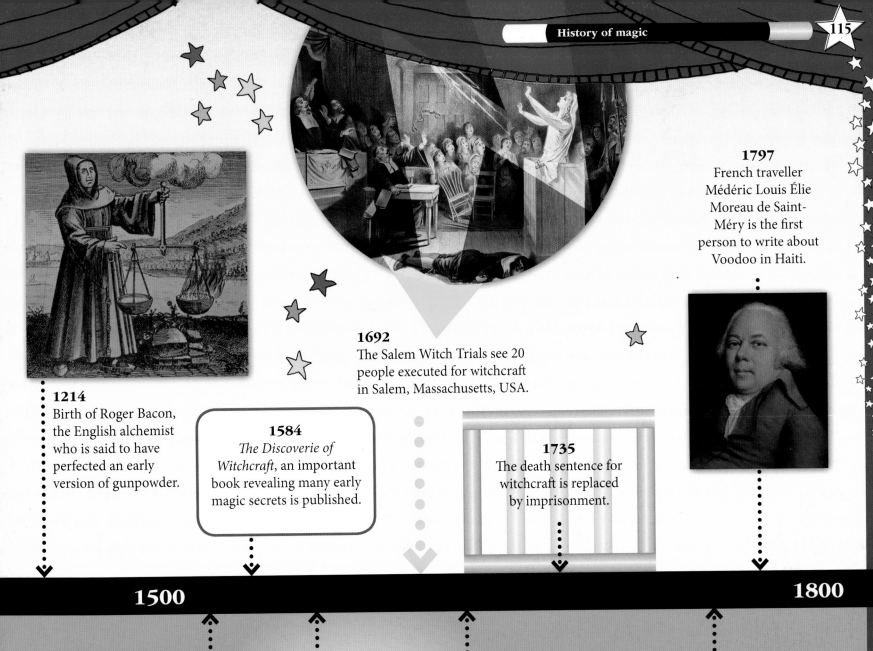

1797
French traveller Médéric Louis Élie Moreau de Saint-Méry is the first person to write about Voodoo in Haiti.

1692
The Salem Witch Trials see 20 people executed for witchcraft in Salem, Massachusetts, USA.

1214
Birth of Roger Bacon, the English alchemist who is said to have perfected an early version of gunpowder.

1584
The Discoverie of Witchcraft, an important book revealing many early magic secrets is published.

1735
The death sentence for witchcraft is replaced by imprisonment.

1500

1800

1606
William Shakespeare writes the play Macbeth, which includes a famous and powerful scene in which the Scottish lord confronts three witches.

1558
John Dee becomes Royal Astrologer to Queen Elizabeth I of England. He later undertakes magic rituals and spells.

1727
Death of Sir Isaac Newton. His family hide his works on alchemy and publish only his works on physics and science.

1750
Joseph Pinetti, a very influential early magician is born.

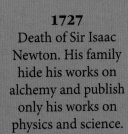

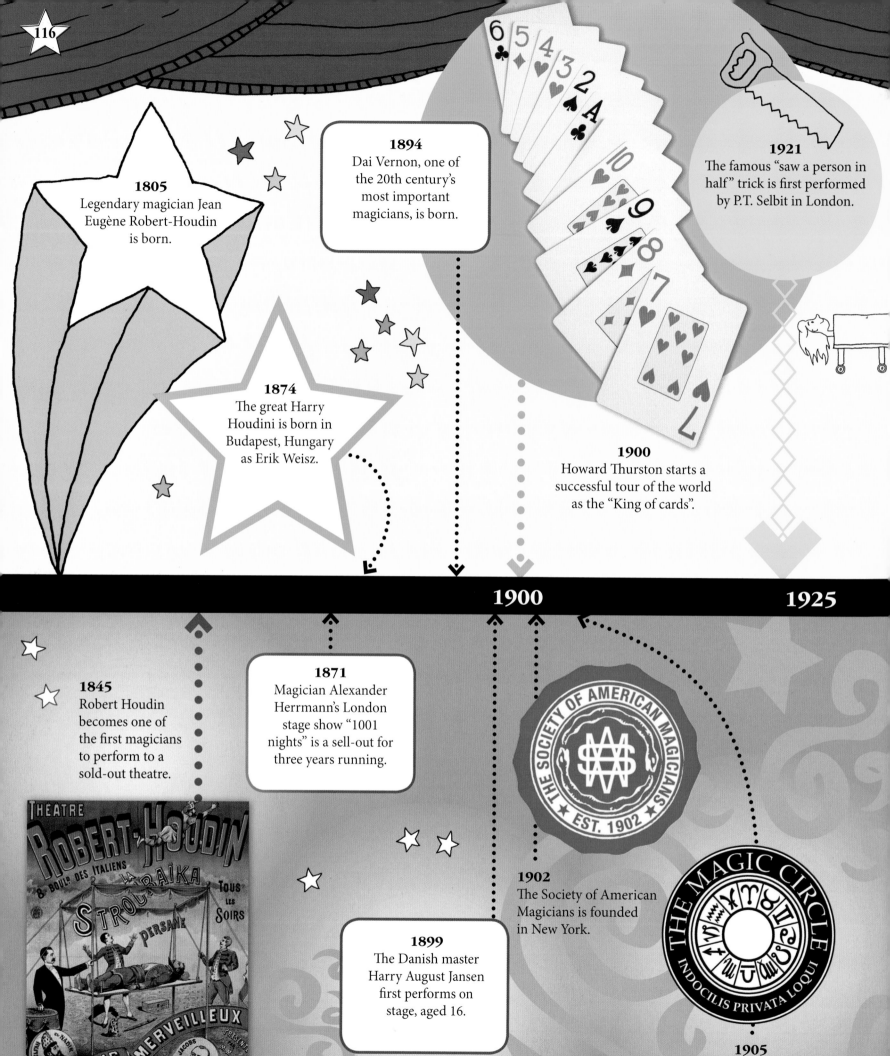

1805
Legendary magician Jean Eugène Robert-Houdin is born.

1894
Dai Vernon, one of the 20th century's most important magicians, is born.

1921
The famous "saw a person in half" trick is first performed by P.T. Selbit in London.

1874
The great Harry Houdini is born in Budapest, Hungary as Erik Weisz.

1900
Howard Thurston starts a successful tour of the world as the "King of cards".

1900   **1925**

1845
Robert Houdin becomes one of the first magicians to perform to a sold-out theatre.

1871
Magician Alexander Herrmann's London stage show "1001 nights" is a sell-out for three years running.

1902
The Society of American Magicians is founded in New York.

1899
The Danish master Harry August Jansen first performs on stage, aged 16.

1905
The Magic Circle is founded in London.

THEATRE ROBERT-HOUDIN
8. BOUL^D. DES ITALIENS
LA KRAÏKA
STROUBAÏKA
PERSANE
TOUS LES SOIRS
TRUC MERVEILLEUX
NOUVEAU
PAR LE PERSAN
DJELFEH-EL-NADIR

THE SOCIETY OF AMERICAN MAGICIANS
★ EST. 1902 ★

THE MAGIC CIRCLE
INDOCILIS PRIVATA LOQUI

1997
The first of the Harry Potter novels, *Harry Potter and the Philosopher's Stone*, is published.

1937
The wizard Gandalf first appears in the novel *The Hobbit* by J.R.R. Tolkein.

1954
English scholar Gerald Gardner publishes his work on what he claims to be the ancient pagan religion of Britain, laying the foundations for the modern Wicca religion.

1980s
The town of Glastonbury in Somerset, England, becomes a centre for New Age philosophy and those living alternative lifestyles.

1950

2000

1963
The Magic Castle is opened as a club and performance venue for magicians in Hollywood, California.

1926
Harry Houdini dies in Detroit, USA. A special broken wand ceremony takes place at his funeral.

1957
American magician David Copperfield is born.

2014
First known all-female group of sadhus is formed in Allahabad, India.

1936
Sir Isaac Newton's works on alchemy are rediscovered and published for the first time.

HIDDEN SKILLS

EVERY MAGICIAN NEEDS

Learning magic can be very rewarding. On top of learning fun and entertaining tricks, magic teaches discipline, hand-eye coordination, and more. But it's not always easy, and there are several hidden skills every magician needs if they want to leave their mark.

YOU WILL NEED

CONFIDENCE

It's important not to forget the "show" in a magic show. But if the magician isn't comfortable and confident while performing their tricks, they run the risk of being forgettable. Good magicians put just as much time into making their shows as **fun as possible**, as they do with their tricks.

DEDICATION

Perhaps the most important skill a magician needs is dedication. Even simple techniques require practice, and difficult ones will need a lot – some take weeks, months, or even years to master. In fact, the greatest magicians can **spend a lifetime** perfecting tricks!

PATIENCE

An impatient magician will be tempted to perform a trick before it has been perfected, but a skilled magician will practice a trick so much they can almost do it **without thinking**. Remember, you only get one chance to impress somebody with a trick, so it's important to make sure you're ready.

SHOWMANSHIP

Learning tricks is one thing, but it takes a while for magicians to perform tricks without stopping to set up each one. The best magicians develop routines that **flow smoothly**. For example, if a trick involves predicting an audience member's card, the next trick could involve using that same card for something else.

HUNGER TO LEARN

No good magician will suddenly decide they have learned everything there is to know. The best ones will always be looking for things to **improve their act** – from the latest equipment, to new and interesting techniques. Just like with any other skill, a master's work is never done.

CREATIVITY

The thing that separates good magicians from great ones is creativity. Once a magician can perform a range of tricks and put together an impressive show, they need to develop their own personal style that **makes them stand out**. Creativity is the sign of a true master.

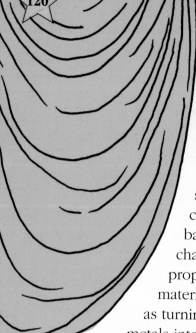

GLOSSARY

Alchemy
A medieval study of chemistry based on changing the properties of materials, such as turning various metals into gold.

Astrology
The practice of studying the movement of stars and planets to see if they have any influence on our lives.

Audience
A group of people gathered together to watch and listen to a show or event.

Conjurer
Another word for a magician.

Cut
A method of separating a deck of cards, often in half, without rearranging their order.

Deal
To take the cards off the top of the deck and arrange them on a table or among several people.

Deck of cards
A standard pack of cards containing 52 playing cards and usually 2 jokers.

Disappearing
Another word for vanishing.

Divination
The ability to predict the future.

Effect
The intended outcome of a magic trick. What the audience thinks they see happening.

Escapology
Performance feats involving escaping from restraints such as ropes or handcuffs.

Future
Events that haven't happened yet.

I Ching
An ancient Chinese practice involving trying to predict the future.

Illusion
Something that looks real but isn't. The word illusion can also be used to describe a large trick.

Levitation
The ability to make something or someone appear to defy gravity by floating or flying.

Magic
The art of entertaining an audience by seeming to use supernatural forces.

Magician
A person who performs a range of magic tricks or illusions to entertain an audience.

Mentalist
A performer that specializes in making it seem like they have the ability to read minds and predict the future.

Misdirection
A set of skills used by a magician to direct the attention of the audience somewhere else while they perform a secret move.

Mysticism
A religious or spiritual belief that knowledge can be gained through prayer or deep thinking.

Occult
Things that are viewed as being supernatural or mystical.

Patter
The words a magician says while performing their tricks. It varies depending on the magician, but it is usually a mixture of stories, jokes, and questions.

Philosopher's stone
A substance alchemists believed could be used to turn metal into gold and grant eternal life.

Prediction
An attempt to judge the outcome of an event before it takes place.

Production
The effect of making an object or person magically appear from out of nowhere.

Prop
Any item or piece of equipment used by a magician in their act.

Prophecy
A prediction about the future that is made through spiritual or religious means.

Restoration
The effect of taking a broken object and fixing it as part of a magic trick.

Routine
A series of tricks or illusions performed one after another.

Ritual
A religious or spiritual ceremony where a set of actions are performed in a certain order.

Shuffle
Rearranging the order of a deck of cards.

Silks
The magician's name for silk handkerchiefs – a prop used in many magic tricks.

Sleight of hand
A set of secret skillful actions used to hide what a magician is really doing in order to complete a trick.

Sorcery
The practice of using magic spells.

Spell
A series of words thought to have supernatural powers.

Stacking the deck
Arranging a deck of cards in a certain order so that it will affect the outcome of a trick.

Stage magic
Tricks designed to be performed in front of a large audience.

Street magic
Tricks performed on the street that usually rely more on a magician's skill with small objects.

Suspension
The effect of keeping an object or person floating in the air. Unlike levitations the object does not rise or fall on its own.

Teleportation
The effect of an object moving to a different place in a seemingly impossible way.

Transformation
The effect of turning one or more objects into something else.

Transposition
An effect similar to teleportation, but where two or more objects switch places.

Trick
An action performed by a magician to entertain an audience.

Vanishing
The effect of making an object or person disappear from sight.

Volunteer
A person from the audience who offers to take part in a trick, but who isn't an assistant.

Wand
A small staff which channels the energy of the magician to make the magic happen. Also commonly used for misdirection.

Witchcraft
The practice of using magic spells or communication with spirits.

Wizard
A person who practices sorcery.

INDEX

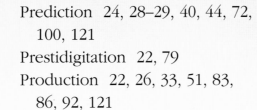

WITH THANKS

The publisher would like to thank the following for their kind permission to reproduce their photographs:

(**Key:** a-above; b-below/bottom; c-centre; f-far; l-left; r-right; t-top)

05 **Dorling Kindersley:** Davenport's Magic Kingdom (bl). 6 **The Library of Congress, Washington DC:** LC-U SZC4-13475. 10 **Corbis:** Reuters (cl); Werner Forman Archive (br). **Getty Images:** Universal Images Group (cra). 11 **Dreamstime.com:** Lefteris Papaulakis (tr). **Getty Images:** De Agostini (b); Hulton Archive (tl). 12 **Corbis:** Patrick Dieudonne / Robert Harding World Imagery (bl); Michael Nicholson (cra). **Dreamstime.com:** Mike Heywood (crb). **Thinkstock:** Photos.com (cla). 13 **The Bridgeman Art Library:** Private Collection (br). **Corbis:** Tiziana and Gianni Baldizzone (ca); Reuters (tr); Michel Setbourn (tl). **Thinkstock:** Richard Waghorn (bl). 14 **akg-images:** (b). **Getty Images:** Hulton Archive (t). 15 **Dreamstime.com:** Shane Larson (cra); Liubov Nazarova (bc). **Photos.com:** (tr). **SuperStock:** Iberfoto (tl). **Thinkstock:** iStock (clb). **Wikipedia:** (br). 16 **Alamy Images:** The Art Archive (cra). **Getty Images:** (br). 17 **Alamy Images:** Interfoto (tr). **Corbis:** Bettmann (tl); Reuters (b). **Dorling Kindersley:** Courtesy of the London Dungeon (c). 18 **Alamy Images:** www.BibleLandPictures.co (tr). **Corbis:** Angelo Cavalli (bl); Massimo Listri (tl). **Glowimages:** ImageBroker (br). 19 **Alamy Images:** Adrian Sherratt (b). **Corbis:** Werner Forman Archive (tl). **Glowimages:** Heritage Images (tr). 20 **Mary Evans Picture Library:** (b). 21 **Corbis:** Bettmann (b). **Getty Images:** (tr). **SuperStock:** Iberfoto (tl). 22 **Glowimages:** Heritage Images (tc). **SuperStock:** Iberfoto (bc). **TopFoto.co.uk:** The Granger Collection (tr). 23 **akg-images:** (tr, tc). **SuperStock:** Iberfoto (b). 26 **Getty Images:** Halfdark (br); Hulton Archive (clb). 27 **Getty Images:** (t). 28 **The Library of Congress, Washington DC:** LC-USZC4-12756 (ca); POS - MAG - .P45 (tl); POS - TH - SPE (b). 29 **Alamy Images: The Protected Art Archive** (br). **Photoshot:** UPPA (tr). **TopFoto.co.uk:** Marilyn Kingwill / ArenaPAL (bl). 31 **The Bridgeman Art Library:** Anthony Southcombe (Contemporary Artist) / Private Collection (cr). 32 **The Bridgeman Art Library:** Peter Newark American Pictures (tl). **Dorling Kindersley:** Davenport's Magic Kingdom (cra). **Dreamstime.com:** 3drenderings (br). **Houston Museum of Natural Science:** (ca). **TopFoto.co.uk:** The Granger Collection (crb). 33 **Dorling Kindersley:** Davenport's Magic Kingdom (clb). **The Art Archive:** Bibliothèque des Arts Décoratifs Paris / Gianni Dagli Orti (br). 35 **The Bridgeman Art Library:** DaTo Images. 47 Mike Caveney's Egyptian Hall Museum. 49 **Dorling Kindersley:** Davenport's Magic Kingdom. 61 **Mike Caveney's Egyptian Hall Museum:** (br). 62 **The Library of Congress, Washington DC:** LC-USZC4-5919 (cr). 63 Dr Timothy Moore, Columbus Ohio. 74 **The Bridgeman Art Library:** Freer Gallery of Art, Smithsonian Institution, USA (fcr); The Stapleton Collection / Private Collection (tl). Getty Images: (bl); The Bridgeman Art Library, London (cr). 75 **Dorling Kindersley:** Davenport's Magic Kingdom. 76 The Library of Congress, Washington DC: LC-DIG-hec-47005 (cr); LC-USZC4-5920 (br). **TopFoto.co.uk:** The Granger Collection (tc). 77 **The Library of Congress, Washington DC:** LC-USZC4-1624. 80 **The International Brotherhood of Magicians, http://www.magician.org, office@magician.org:** (c). **The London Society of Magicians:** (b). ™ **The Magic Circle:** (ca). **The Society of American Magicians www.magicsam.com:** (cb). 81 Getty Images. 94 **Dorling Kindersley:** Davenport's Magic Kingdom (tc, c). **Getty Images:** (bc). 95 **Dorling Kindersley:** Davenport's Magic Kingdom (cr, bl). **The Library of Congress, Washington DC:** LC-DIG-ppmsca-23992 (tl); LC-USZ62-110548 (tc); LC-USZ62-66403 (tr). 106 **Alamy Images:** Mooziic (tc). **Artscape Galleries:** (cr). **Getty Images:** Hulton Archive (bc). 107 **Alamy Images:** The Protected Art Archive. 110 **Corbis:** Bettmann (cl). **Getty Images:** Barcroft Media (cr). **Jeff Sheridan Archives:** (bl). 111 **Corbis:** EPA. 112 **Alamy Images:** Elizabeth Leyden (cl); Arch White (b). 113 **Alamy Images:** Creative Control (t). **Getty Images:** (b). 114 **Corbis:** (cla). **Getty Images:** Hulton Archive (cra). **Glowimages:** Heritage Images (br, bl). 115 **Alamy Images:** Interfoto (cla). **Getty Images:** British Library / Robana (br). **Photo Scala, Florence:** The Metropolitan Museum of Art / Art Resource (cra). **The Library of Congress, Washington DC:** LC-DIG-ppmsca-09402 (tc). **Thinkstock:** Photos.com (clb). 116 **SuperStock:** Iberfoto (bl). 117 **Alamy Images:** Sunil Malhotra (br); Photos 12 (tl). **TopFoto.co.uk:** Charles Walker (tc)

Jacket images: Front: 123RF.com: Igor Zhuravlov / NASA / JPL-Caltech (Lenticular / sky); **Dreamstime.com:** Mariia Pazhyna / Mpagina (Lenticular / top hat); **Getty Images:** Halfdark (Lenticular / rabbit); **Back: Dorling Kindersley:** Davenport's Magic Kingdom cla; **Getty Images:** Halfdark ca; **Spine: Dorling Kindersley:** Davenport's Magic Kingdom (wand), (flowers)

All other images © Dorling Kindersley
For further information see: www.dkimages.com

With thanks to:
Davenport's Magic Kingdom

The Davenport's are a family of fourth generation magicians, and their expertise and contributions throughout the publication of this book have been greatly appreciated. Their family-owned museum and theatre in the UK celebrates the history of magical entertainment with exhibitions and events.

Dorling Kindersley would also like to thank:

Sasha Gray, Peter Lock, Jane Mistry, Kiran Mistry, and James Wilson for modelling. Deborah Lock and Katie Federico for assistance with the photo shoots. Candice and Jeff Sheridan, The International Brotherhood of Magicians, The London Society of Magicians, The Magic Circle, and The Society of American Magicians for their kind contributions. Margaret Parrish for Americanization, and Claire Bowers and Claire Cordier for picture library assistance.